D0950760

שערי מצוה

GATES OF MITZVAH

Direct me in the path of Your *mitzvot,*
for I delight in it.

—PSALMS 119:35

שערי מצוה

GATES OF MITZVAH

A Guide to the Jewish Life Cycle

Edited by
Simeon J. Maslin

Illustrated by Ismar David

CENTRAL CONFERENCE OF AMERICAN RABBIS

5739 NEW YORK 1979

All Rights Reserved
Copyright © 1979, Central Conference of American Rabbis, New York
Library of Congress Catalog Card Number: 78-20790
Printed in the U.S.A.
Fourth Printing, 1991

LIBRARY OF CONGRESS CATALOGING IN PUBLICATION DATA
Main entry under title:

In English. שערי מצוה
Includes bibliographical references and index.
    I.   Reform Judaism—Ceremonies and practices.
2.   Commandments (Judaism)   I.   Maslin, Simeon J.
II.   Central Conference of American Rabbis.   Committee
on Reform Jewish Practice.   III.   Title: Gates of
mitzvah.   IV.   Title: Shaarei mitzvah.

BM197.S45   296.7'4   78-20790
ISBN 0-916694-37-2
ISBN 0-916694-53-4 pbk.

This book was produced by the Committee on Reform Jewish
Practice of the Central Conference of American Rabbis
W. Gunther Plaut, *Chairman*

Herbert M. Baumgard	Herman E. Schaalman
Peter S. Knobel	Richard F. Steinbrink
Simeon J. Maslin	Michael Stroh

Publications Working Committee

Bennett M. Hermann	Brooks R. Susman

Ex Officio

A. Stanley Dreyfus	Walter Jacob

Jacket art: Laura Stevens   Book designer: Ernst Reichl

This book is dedicated
with love and gratitude to
מורנו ורבנו
SOLOMON B. FREEHOF
whose devotion to God, Torah and Israel
has been a source of enlightenment
and inspiration.
ברוך שחלק מחכמתו ליריאיו
"Blessed be He who has imparted of His wisdom
to them that revere Him."
—Berachot 58a

CONTENTS

FOREWORD

In 1972 the Central Conference of American Rabbis published *A Shabbat Manual*, designed to intensify Jewish observance in the home. The Conference began with Shabbat and now, in this new volume, turns to life-cycle events. It is hoped that a third volume dealing with Holy Days and ethical commitments will follow in the not too distant future.

The publication of this book proceeds from the knowledge that Judaism was never meant to be merely an institutional religion. Its ultimate focus remains the individual, in personal observance and personal deed, at home and at work. Our religion urges us, on our journey from life to death, to give continual expression to our belief in God and in the significance of our membership in the historic people. This volume aims at helping each individual Jew to make Jewish decisions in his or her life. It sets out guideposts for making such decisions; the rest is up to each person.

Shaarei Mitzvah is the result of several years of labor by the Committee on Reform Jewish Practice which was helped by suggestions made by scores of Conference members. In many ways, however, *Shaarei Mitzvah* is the special creation of its editor, Rabbi Simeon J. Maslin, without whose singular devotion it would not have been published. All of us owe him profound and abiding gratitude. In addition, special essays on the meaning of *mitzvah* have been contributed by Rabbis Roland B. Gittelsohn, Arthur J. Lelyveld, David Polish and Herman E. Schaalman and brief essays expanding on ideas in the main body of the book were written by members of the Committee and Rabbis Herbert Bronstein and Mark L. Winer. A special word of thanks to Joseph B. Glaser and Elliot L. Stevens for their devoted assistance in the preparation of this book. For all of them, the greatest reward will be an increase in Jewish observance and commitment

on the part of those to whom the book is directed. As the ancient saying
has it: "The reward of a *mitzvah* is the *mitzvah* itself."

W. GUNTHER PLAUT, CHAIRMAN,
Committee on Reform Jewish Practice

Tevet, 5739
January, 1979

BEHOLD DO NOT
A GOOD DOCTRINE FORSAKE IT
HAS BEEN GIVEN YOU

IT IS A TREE OF LIFE FOR THOSE WHO HOLD IT FAST

RELIGIOUS PRACTICE

Judaism emphasizes action rather than creed as the primary expression of a religious life, the means by which we strive to achieve universal justice and peace. Reform Judaism shares this emphasis on duty and obligation. Our founders stressed that the Jew's ethical responsibilities, personal and social, are enjoined by God. The past century has taught us that the claims made upon us may begin with our ethical obligations, but they extend to many other aspects of Jewish living, including creating a Jewish home centered on family devotion, lifelong study, private prayer and public worship, daily religious observance, keeping the Sabbath and the holy days, celebrating the major events of life, involvement with the synagogue and community, and other activities which promote the survival of the Jewish people and enhance its existence. Within each area of Jewish observance, Reform Jews are called upon to confront the claims of Jewish tradition, however differently perceived, and to exercise their individual autonomy, choosing and creating on the basis of commitment and knowledge.

—From the "Centenary Perspective,"
adopted by the Central Conference
of American Rabbis, 1976.

INTRODUCTION

THERE is a classic story about a man who set off in search of a treasure. When, at last, he came upon the secret place where it was hidden, he found that the place was his own home. The treasure had been in his possession all along.

This book proceeds from the belief that the treasure of Jewish living is within the reach of everyone. It has been written to help searching Jews rediscover the treasure of *mitzvah* which is theirs.

Mitzvah is the key to authentic Jewish existence and to the sanctification of life.* No English equivalent can adequately translate the term. Its root meaning is "commandment," but *mitzvah* has come to have broader meanings. It suggests the joy of doing something for the sake of others and for the sake of God, and it conveys still more: it also speaks of living Jewishly, of meeting life's challenges and opportunities in particular ways. All this is *mitzvah*. Doing one *mitzvah*, says our tradition, will lead us to do another and another.

This book was written by Reform rabbis. Reform Judaism attempts responses to the conditions of each age in order to make it possible for Jews to live their Judaism meaningfully and richly. Such Jewish responses should seek to preserve the continuity of Jewish life and at the same time be sensitive to opportunities for desirable innovation.

In an earlier stage, Reform sought to distinguish between ethical and ritual *mitzvot*. It was argued that the ethical commandments were valid eternally and thus binding upon Jews of every generation. The ritual

---

* Four essays appended to this book set forth different points of view on why, how, and to what extent a modern Jew may feel required to perform *mitzvot*, as well as on the place of ethics in the Jewish system of *mitzvot*. A careful study of these essays will help the reader to develop a personal rationale through which the performance of a *mitzvah* may become meaningful.

commandments, however, were considered linked to particular experiences or circumstances, and therefore they were considered optional or even superfluous. But this dichotomy is often arbitrary, for ethical resolve and ritual expression, intention and act, are in fact closely interlinked, as are reason and feeling. Ritual, as the vehicle for confronting God and Jewish history, can shape and stimulate one's ethical impulses. Therefore, the ancient advice is still valid: the very act of doing a *mitzvah* may lead one to know the heart of the matter.

This book was conceived to help Jews make *Jewish* responses, to give their lives *Jewish* depth and character. It recognizes that not all Jews need to do the same thing or make the same responses, that even within the realm of each *mitzvah* various levels of doing or understanding might exist. Reform Judaism maintains the principle of individual freedom; each Jew must make a personal decision about the Judaism which has come down through the ages. Nevertheless all Jews who acknowledge themselves to be members of their people and its tradition thereby limit their freedom to some extent. This book is an expression of Reform Jewish philosophy in that it is built on the twin commitments which each Jew ought to have, the commitments to Jewish continuity and to personal freedom of choice.

Certain *mitzvot* are included in this book and others are not. In some areas new *mitzvot* are suggested. But the processes of selectivity and innovation in the creation of this book were never arbitrary. The authors did what they hoped all Jews might do: they studied Jewish tradition first and foremost and, on the basis of such study, made choices with regard to existing *mitzvot*. Where they felt that long-standing practices and customs responded to the needs of our time, they gave them strong and urgent support. Where they felt—as, for instance, in matters regarding the equality of men and women—that new means were needed to express religious needs, they did not hesitate to suggest alternative *mitzvot*. But they always began with a consideration of those *mitzvot* which had been observed for generations and which they felt must remain the starting points on this Jewish journey.

Shaarei Mitzvah is a guide to doing, and it is also a reminder that *kavvanah*—intention, will, devotion—is vital. *Kavvanah* is, in fact, at the core of *mitzvot;* it is the motivation which enables a person to begin making choices. The easy path is to do only that which is convenient, but living Jewishly is not and has never been identical with convenience. A *mitzvah* which might be inconvenient and even awkward at first can, with patience and practice, take on deep personal significance and provide moments of sacred meeting.*

Some may read this book and decide that the *mitzvot* suggested are too many or too demanding. But a few *mitzvot* observed with *kavvanah* will lead to an enlargement of commitment as time goes on. The secret of observing *mitzvot* is to begin.

---

* There are people who, for a variety of personal reasons, may not be able to perform certain *mitzvot* suggested in this book. The *mitzvot* of the Jewish home, for example, traditionally revolve around the family, yet today the number of single adults and single parents in Jewish communities is increasing and altering the definition of "living Jewishly" (see "The Single Person, The Single-Parent Family, and *Mitzvot*," page 119). While the performance and application of certain *mitzvot* may differ due to personal circumstances, the principles which undergird them apply to all Jews.

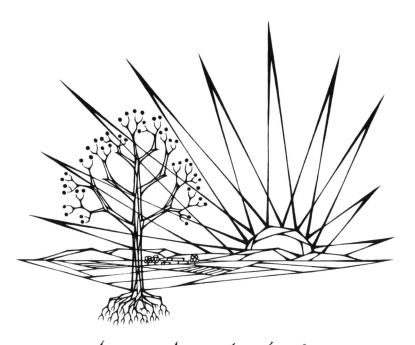

BIRTH

CHILDHOOD
and EDUCATION

God created the human being
    in His own image. . . .
male and female He created them.
And God blessed them.
                    —GENESIS 1:27–28

Be fruitful and multiply:
A nation, yea, an assembly of nations,
Shall descend from you.
                    —GENESIS 35:11

Set these words, which I
command you this day, upon your heart.
Teach them faithfully to your children.
              —DEUTERONOMY 6:6–7

THE first commandment in the Torah is "*Peru u-revu*—Be fruitful and multiply" (Genesis 1:28). Judaism has always regarded children as a blessing from God and the procreation of children as a *mitzvah*. Jews have seen their progeny as evidence of their love and as assurance of the continued existence of the Jewish people. This last consideration has increased in importance since the Holocaust and the annihilation of one-third of the Jewish people.

The Bible teaches that each birth is a God-blessed event. In Genesis we read that God said to Abraham: "I will bless her [Sarah]; indeed, I will give you a son by her" (17:16). Since earliest times Jews have felt that there is an element of the sacred in each birth, that is, that procreation involves more than sexual intercourse and conception. The Bible is not vague or evasive as to the biological preconditions for birth: "Now the man knew his wife Eve, and she conceived and bore Cain," but when Eve gave Cain his name, she acknowledged "the help of the Lord" (Genesis 4:1). In the biblical tradition God was always present as the essential third partner in the process of procreation.

Modern Jews, too, believe that there are spiritual dimensions to the birth of a child and that the blessing of parenthood should be shared with the entire community. Every child born of Jewish parents is a part of the Jewish community, and the community shares in the responsibility of raising the child.[1] There are no greater communal joys than the *berit* and the baby-naming, for every Jewish child bears the seed of Jewish survival.

It is a fundamental principle of Judaism that every child is created pure, in the divine image.[2] The first chapters of Genesis state repeatedly that the human being is fashioned "in the image of God" (1:26, 27; 5:1, 3; 9:6), implying that the child is born with the potential of growth toward ideal love, creativity, justice, and mercy. Jewish parents have a crucial responsibility to raise their children so that they will be capable of wise and moral choices.

Consequently, Judaism has developed certain traditions surrounding the birth of a child and the formative years.

A. *BIRTH*

A-1 The *mitzvah* of procreation

It is a *mitzvah* for a man and a woman, recognizing the sanctity of life and the sanctity of the marriage partnership, to bring children into the world.[3] *

A-2 Birth control

Reform Judaism respects the right of parents to determine how many children they should have. In considering family size, however, parents should be aware of the tragic decimation of our people during the Holocaust and of the threats of annihilation that have pursued the Jewish people through history. Thus, while Reform Judaism approves of the practice of birth control, couples are encouraged to consider the matter of family size carefully and with due regard to the problem of Jewish survival.[4]

A-3 Abortion

In keeping with the fundamental principle of the sanctity of life, Judaism has since ancient times allowed and even prescribed abortion in cases where the life or health of the mother is in danger.[5] In keeping with this tradition, and recognizing that one's emotional health is as important as one's physical health, Reform Judaism affirms the right of a woman, after due regard to the sanctity of life and in accordance with the principles of Jewish morality, to determine whether or not she can continue

---

* There are people who, for a variety of valid reasons, will be unable to fulfil this *mitzvah*. It should be understood that any *mitzvah* prescribed in this book is a *mitzvah* only for those who are physically and emotionally capable of fulfilling it. Those who cannot are considered no less observant and no less Jewish.

a pregnancy to term.[6] Abortion may be medically indicated in cases where genetic disease or malformation of the fetus is probable. In all such cases the mother and father should consult with their rabbi (see "Marriage," A-4).

A-4 The *mitzvah* of adoption

It is a *mitzvah* equal to procreation to adopt children and provide them with the benefits of home, family, and education (see D).[7]

A-5 The *mitzvah* of prayer after childbirth

It is a *mitzvah* for parents to join in a prayer of gratitude as soon as possible after the child's birth. Science alone cannot comprehend the mystery of human birth and the wonder of parenthood. The experience of childbirth should help people realize that they are part of an eternal process which transcends them.[8]

שֶׁהֶחֱיָנוּ   The prayer *She-heche-yanu* is particularly appropriate:

בָּרוּךְ אַתָּה, יְיָ אֱלֹהֵינוּ, מֶלֶךְ הָעוֹלָם,
שֶׁהֶחֱיָנוּ וְקִיְּמָנוּ וְהִגִּיעָנוּ
לַזְּמַן הַזֶּה.

**Ba-ruch a-ta, A-do-nai E-lo-hei-nu, me-lech ha-o-lam,
she-he-che-ya-nu ve-ki-ye-ma-nu ve-hi-gi-a-nu
la-ze-man ha-zeh.**

*Blessed is the Lord our God, Ruler of the universe,
for giving us life, for sustaining us, and for enabling
us to reach this joyous occasion.*

Other prayers for parents and grandparents may be found in *Gates of the House*, pages 109–10.

A-6   The *mitzvah* of *tzedakah*

צְדָקָה   It is a *mitzvah* to make a gift of *tzedakah*[9] in honor of
the birth of one's child. A gift to the synagogue and particularly to the religious school is appropriate. In keeping
with the ancient tradition of planting trees to celebrate
the birth of children,[10] the purchase of trees in Israel is
also suggested.

B. *ENTERING THE COVENANT*

B-1   The *mitzvah* of *berit*

It is a *mitzvah* for every Jewish child to be brought into
the covenant community with prayer and appropriate
ritual.

בְּרִית   The Jewish people is a covenant (*berit*) community,
as we read in the Torah: " 'If you will obey Me faithfully
and keep My covenant, you shall be My treasured possession among all the peoples. Indeed, all the world is
Mine, but you shall be to Me a kingdom of priests and a
holy nation.' . . . And all the people answered as one,
saying: 'All that the Lord has spoken, we will do!' "
(Exodus 19:5–8).

Jewish tradition is specific about the fact that both
men *and* women entered into the Sinaitic *berit* with
God.[11] And so, even though the word *berit* has come to
be associated with the circumcision of Jewish male children since the days of Abraham (Genesis 17:9–14), it
should be understood that every child born into the
Jewish people, male or female, is a part of the *berit*.

B-2   The *mitzvah* of circumcision

Ancient tradition prescribes the method by which a male
child is brought into the covenant, as we read in the

Torah: "God said to Abraham: 'As for you, you shall keep My covenant [*berit*], you and your offspring to come, throughout the ages. Such is the covenant which you shall keep, between Me and you and your offspring to follow: every male among you shall be circumcised . . .'" (Genesis 17:9–10). It is, therefore, a *mitzvah* to bring a male child into the covenant through the rite of circumcision—*berit milah.*

בְּרִית מִילָה   *Berit milah* is, however, more than a surgical procedure. It should be performed as a symbolic binding of one's son to the covenant community. Circumcision alone, without the appropriate prayers, does not constitute entrance into the covenant. The *berit milah* service may be found in *Gates of the House,* pages 111–13.

B-3 The *mitzvah* of circumcision on the eighth day

It is a *mitzvah* to circumcise a male child on the eighth day, as we read in the Torah: "At the age of eight days every male among you throughout the generations shall be circumcised" (Genesis 17:12). So significant is the *mitzvah* of circumcision on the *eighth* day that tradition requires the performance of the ceremony on that day even if it falls on Shabbat or Yom Kippur. In cases where this is not possible, the rabbi should be consulted.

Circumcision may be postponed for medical reasons. If postponed, it should be held as soon as possible consistent with the health of the child. In the case of hemophilia or any other medical contraindication, circumcision may be indefinitely postponed. In such cases parents should arrange for appropriate prayers (as in the case of females; see B-6) initiating their son into the covenant community. Such an uncircumcised Jewish male is considered a full member of the Jewish people and a participant in the *berit.*

B-4 The joy of the *mitzvah*

Parents are encouraged to share the joy of the *berit milah* service with family and friends.[12] This service is held most appropriately in the home but may also be held in the synagogue or in the hospital, depending upon the wishes of the family and the facilities available.

B-5 The officiant at *berit milah*

In keeping with the sacred nature of *berit milah*, parents are encouraged to consult with the rabbi about the ceremony. Whenever possible, *berit milah* should be performed by a person specially trained, both religiously מוֹהֵל and medically, in this procedure, a *mohel*.[13] If a *mohel* is not available or if the parents prefer that a doctor perform the operation, one should be selected who is Jewish, who is familiar with the ritual of *berit milah*, and who will do the surgical procedure with due regard for the sanctity of the occasion.

When neither a *mohel* nor a Jewish doctor is available, a non-Jewish doctor may be used, but it is the responsibility of the parents to explain to the doctor that the circumcision is being done for religious reasons and to arrange for the proper prayers to be offered (see B-2).

B-6 A *berit* service for girls

It is a *mitzvah* to bring daughters as well as sons into the *berit*. Reform Judaism is committed to the equality of the sexes, and in consonance with this principle, parents should arrange a *berit* service for girls either at home or in the synagogue. A *berit* service for girls—The Covenant of Life—may be found in *Gates of the House*, pages 114–17.

B-7   Parents' role in the *berit*

The responsibility for bringing a child into the *berit* rests upon its parents. Traditionally, it was the father who was required to circumcise his son or to present him to the *mohel* for circumcision. In Reform Judaism parents share the responsibility for bringing their sons and daughters into the *berit*, and both mothers and fathers are involved in the ceremonies. The parents' declarations and prayers may be found in *Gates of the House*, pages 111–17.

B-8   *Berit* customs

Several customs involving grandparents and/or honored friends have evolved over the centuries and have become a part of the *berit* ceremony in various communities. One of these is the appointment of a *sandek* (the person who is given the honor of holding the child during the operation); another is the appointment of a *kwater* and a *kwaterin* (godfather and godmother) to present the child to the *mohel*.[14] The rabbi should be consulted about these customs.

C.   NAMING THE CHILD

C-1   The *mitzvah* of naming a child

It is a *mitzvah* to give a child a Hebrew name.[15] This name should be announced and the child blessed in the synagogue. The naming ceremony usually takes place at a regular Sabbath or daily service at the earliest time after the birth of the child when both parents can attend. It is recommended that this ceremony be held within two months of birth.

It was customary to link the name of the child with that of the father through the connecting Hebrew words בֵּן ... בַּת *ben* (son of) or *bat* (daughter of), e.g., Yosef *ben* Daniel. In Reform Judaism, however, it is proper to link the name of the child with both mother and father, e.g., Yosef *ben* Rachel *ve*-Daniel.

C-2 Naming in the synagogue

Both boys and girls should be named in the synagogue. If there has been no prior ceremony for a girl marking her entrance into the *berit* (see B-6), the naming ceremony should include a reference to the *berit* and may thus serve both purposes. A naming ceremony for a boy does not serve as a substitute for circumcision (except in such cases as described in B-3).

בְּרִית

C-3 The choice of a name

One should consult with the rabbi about the choice of an appropriate Hebrew or Jewish name. Different communities follow various customs as to the propriety of naming a child after a living relative or, if after a deceased relative, which one. There is no objection in Reform Judaism to naming a child after a living person.[16] Such decisions should be left to the parents; controversy over the choice of names should not be allowed to mar the joy of the naming.

However, a name should be chosen with sensitivity and with the realization that the child will generally have to carry it through life.[17] Parents should realize that the choice of a name is often symbolic of one's aspirations for the child, whether by naming him/her after a particularly beloved or praiseworthy person or by the choice of a name with a particular meaning.

C-4 · The joy of the *mitzvah*

קִדּוּשׁ

עֹנֶג שַׁבָּת

It is a *mitzvah* for parents to share their joy on the occasion of the naming of a child. This may be accomplished by inviting the congregation to join the family in a *kiddush* or an *oneg Shabbat* following the service and naming ceremony.[18]

C-5 Pidyon ha-ben

פִּדְיוֹן הַבֵּן

The ritual of *pidyon ha-ben* (redemption of the first-born son)[19] is generally not observed in Reform congregations.

D. *ADOPTED CHILDREN*

D-1 The *mitzvah* of adoption

מִצְוֹת

All the *mitzvot* and traditions that apply to one's natural children apply equally to adopted children. (see A-4 especially and pertinent sections of A, B, and C above).

D-2 Naming and *berit*

בְּרִית

An adopted child should be named in the synagogue and entered into the *berit* as soon as the initial legal procedures for adoption have been completed.[20] If a male child is not an infant, the rabbi should be consulted about the circumcision.

D-3 Entry into Judaism

If the adopted child is not an infant and was born of non-Jewish or undetermined parents, the rabbi should be consulted as to the procedure for formal entry into the Jewish community.

E. *RAISING AND EDUCATING A JEWISH CHILD*

E-1   The *mitzvah* of *Talmud Torah*

It is a *mitzvah* to teach one's child the traditions and beliefs of Judaism, as it says in the Torah: "Set these words, which I command you this day, upon your heart. Teach them faithfully to your children; speak of them in your home and on your way . . . " (Deuteronomy 6:6–7). This *mitzvah* is called *Talmud Torah*.

תַּלְמוּד תּוֹרָה

E-2   The partnership of synagogue and home

In the raising of a Jewish child, responsibility is shared by the family and the Jewish community. It is up to the family to provide the child with the proper atmosphere for both physical and spiritual growth, and it is up to the community to provide the institutions and the personnel for formal education and celebration of Sabbaths, festivals, and life-cycle events.

Therefore, Jewish parents should live and celebrate their Judaism at home[21] as well as in the synagogue, and should impress upon the children their own commitment to Judaism and the Jewish people through active membership in a congregation, prayer, discussion of topics of Jewish concern, *tzedakah*, the purchase of Jewish books and periodicals, enrollment in synagogue adult classes, and other means of involvement in the life of the Jewish community (see Marriage, section E).

צְדָקָה

Since the synagogue is a democratic institution, it is the responsibility of Jewish parents to see to it that their congregation provides the proper environment for inspiring Jewish worship and education.

E-3 The *mitzvah* of congregational prayer

> It is a *mitzvah* to integrate children into the life of the congregation. As soon as they are old enough, children should be brought to services and encouraged to sit with their parents and participate. When the congregation has "family services," the family should attend together.

E-4 Religious education

> Children should be enrolled in the congregational school as soon as they are eligible. Many congregations mark the beginning of religious education through a Simchat Torah consecration or some other ceremony designed to impress the child with the importance of entrance into the religious school.
>
> Parents should make every effort to help their children understand the importance of religious education. They can best accomplish this by bringing (rather than merely sending) their children to the religious school and by participating in whatever classes, services, or meetings the congregation might provide for adults.

E-5 The *mitzvah* of teaching

> Just as it is a *mitzvah* to teach the beliefs and traditions of Judaism to one's own children, it is equally a *mitzvah* to teach Judaism to the children of the community. Jewish tradition ascribes to a child's teacher the same sacred status as it does to the parents.[22]

E-6 The *mitzvah* of learning Hebrew

> It is a *mitzvah* to learn and teach the Hebrew language.[23] Hebrew is a vital link between Jews and their history and between Jews all over the world and the people of Israel. It is the key to a deeper understanding of the Torah and the other sources of Judaism.

E-7   The *mitzvot* of *aliyah* to the Torah and *Bar/Bat Mitzvah*

עֲלִיָה

בַּר מִצְוָה

בַּת מִצְוָה

קִדּוּשׁ

סְעֻדַּת מִצְוָה

It is a *mitzvah* to be called to the reading of the Torah and to recite the appropriate blessings.[24] This is called an *aliyah* (lit. "going up") and takes place for the first time when the child reaches the age of thirteen and thus becomes a *Bar Mitzvah* or a *Bat Mitzvah*.[25]

The *Bar/Bat Mitzvah* ceremony is a meaningful and traditional way to mark the beginning of puberty and the accomplishment of a degree of Hebrew proficiency. Parents should emphasize the sanctity of the occasion and should not demean it by undue emphasis on the social aspects of the celebration. While *ḳiddush* and the sharing of a festival meal (*se-udat mitzvah*)[18] are customs of long standing, ostentation and lavish display should be avoided. The sanctity of the day can be enhanced for the celebrant and his/her parents through a generous act of *tzedaḳah*.

While the goal of Hebrew language study should not be *Bar/Bat Mitzvah*, this ceremony is generally reserved for those religious-school children who have studied Hebrew and are capable of reading a passage from the Torah. Under no circumstances should *Bar/Bat Mitzvah* mark the conclusion of a child's Jewish education. Parents should help their children understand the richness and vastness of the Jewish heritage and the obligation to continue formal Jewish education through confirmation and, where available, through high school.

E-8   The *mitzvah* of Confirmation

It is a *mitzvah* to be confirmed in the Jewish religion as a member of the Jewish people. Originally, the ceremony of Confirmation was established by the Reform movement as a means of educating young women equally with young men and keeping both in the process of Jewish education beyond the age of thirteen.

The age for Confirmation varies in different congregations, but at whatever age it is held, it should not mark the end point of one's Jewish education. Its purpose is to encourage the intellectual and spiritual growth of young people, to strengthen the bonds between them and the Israelites who received the Torah at Sinai (Exodus 19:3–8 and Deuteronomy 29:9–14), and to stimulate their love for God and the Jewish people.

F. ADULT EDUCATION AND CONVERSION

F-1 The *mitzvah* of study for adults

תַּלְמוּד תּוֹרָה   The *mitzvah* of *Talmud Torah* (see E-1) is incumbent upon every Jew throughout life,[26] whether or not one acquired a Jewish education during childhood.

F-2 Adult *Bar/Bat Mitzvah* and Confirmation

בַּר / בַּת מִצְוָה   Adults who have not celebrated *Bar/Bat Mitzvah* or Confirmation but who are involved in continuing Jewish education should consult with their rabbis as to the possibility of celebrating these joyous *mitzvot* in later life.

F-3 Family *Talmud Torah*

The essential *mitzvot* of *Talmud Torah* for children and for adults may be observed most effectively when they are interlinked, e.g., when parents bring their children to religious school and then attend adult classes or lectures (see E-4), when parents and children attend a Shabbat program or weekend retreat together, or when the family sets aside a regular hour for Jewish study together in the home.

F-4   The *mitzvah* of admitting converts

It is a *mitzvah* to admit into the Jewish community any person who wishes sincerely to adopt Judaism and who is willing to study it and accept its *mitzvot*.[27] Such a person is called a *ger* (masculine form) or a *giyoret* (feminine)—a proselyte or convert.[28]

גֵּר

גִּיֹרֶת

גֵּרִים

The Jewish people have accepted *gerim* (proselytes) since biblical times. Ruth, the great-grandmother of King David, was a Moabite, and it was she who first enunciated the standard for entry into Judaism: "your people shall be my people, and your God my God" (Ruth 1:16).[29]

F-5   The process of *giur*

גִּיוּר

The process of conversion (*giur*) varies from community to community (see page 146 for the full statement on "Admission of Converts" by the CCAR). In Reform Judaism the primary element in conversion is a wholehearted commitment to the Jewish people, its faith, customs, history, and destiny. Usually an intensive course of study is prescribed, along with periodic meetings with the sponsoring rabbi, regular attendance at Shabbat and holy day services, and participation in congregational and community functions and home observances.

A convert may be accepted into the Jewish people at a public service or at a special private service arranged by the rabbi.

F-6   The *mitzvah* of self-acceptance

It is a *mitzvah* for a convert to consider him/herself as one who is totally Jewish, descended from Abraham and Sarah and from ancestors who entered into covenant with God at Sinai (see F-8).[30]

F-7   The *mitzvah* of welcoming converts

It is a *mitzvah* for born Jews to accept converts as equal members of the Jewish community, to make no distinctions between converts and themselves,[31] and to welcome them into the congregation and community.

F-8   Adding a Hebrew name

בֶּן/בַּת

It is customary for a convert to add a Hebrew name to his/her legal name as a symbol of identification with the Jewish people.[32] Added to the name is the traditional designation *ben/bat* (son/daughter of) *Abraham ve-Sarah.*

MARRIAGE

and THE JEWISH HOME

Hence a man leaves his father and mother and clings to his wife, so that they become one flesh.

—GENESIS 2:24

Unless the Lord builds the house,
Its builders labor in vain.

—PSALMS 127:1

Let me be a seal upon your heart,
Like a seal upon your arm,
For love is strong as death . . .
Vast floods cannot quench love,
Nor rivers drown it.

—SONG OF SONGS 8:6–7

A RABBINIC parable tells of a confrontation between a skeptical Roman matron and Rabbi Yose ben Chalafta (2nd cent.).[33] The woman asked the rabbi: "In how many days did God create the world?"

"In six days," he answered.

"Then what has He been doing since then?" she asked.

"He sits and makes marriages," he answered, "assigning this man to that woman and this woman to that man."

The story goes on to describe how the matron, unimpressed by the image of God as a cosmic matchmaker, married off her slaves, two by two, claiming that she could do the same as Rabbi Yose's God. But the next day there was pandemonium in the Roman villa, bruised bodies, complaints and protests, until finally the matron relented. She summoned Rabbi Yose and admitted: "There is no god like your God."

The story is, of course, fanciful, but it gets to the heart of an ancient Jewish belief: that God is involved in marriage, going back to the very beginning of time, to the allegory of the lonely Adam in the Garden of Eden. God takes pity on Adam and says: "It is not good for man to be alone; I will make a partner for him" (Genesis 2:18). The story also implies that finding an appropriate life's companion is no easy matter, and that to do it well might even require divine wisdom.

The traditional Hebrew word for marriage is *Kiddushin*. It is derived from *kadosh*—holy—and this describes quite accurately the Jewish attitude toward marriage (see the essay on *Kiddushin* in the Appendix, p. 123). The Bible describes marriage as the natural state intended by God. "Hence a man leaves his father and mother and clings to his wife, so that they become one flesh" (Genesis 2:24). And the rabbis went further: "He who is without a wife dwells without blessings, life, joy, help, good, and peace."[34]

The degree of holiness that Judaism ascribes to marriage is attested by the tradition that God can be present in the marriage partnership: "When husband and wife are worthy, the Divine Presence abides with them."[35] The idea that the bond of marriage is sacred and eternal, a reflection of the *berit* between God and the people Israel, goes back to the Bible, particularly to the prophecies of Jeremiah (2:2), Ezekiel (16:6–8), and Hosea (2:2–20). And in the Middle Ages the mystic poets of Safed embellished the Shabbat liturgy with the image of joyous conjugal union as a symbol of the *berit* between God and Israel.[36]

It is in this tradition of sacred covenant that a man and a woman are inspired to build together the *mikdash me-at*—the miniature sanctuary—that the Jewish home should be, a place of serenity sanctified daily by the performance of *mitzvot*. In such an atmosphere a man and a woman can raise children capable of absorbing the traditions of Judaism so that Israel may survive eternally as a "kingdom of priests and a holy people" (Exodus 19:6). Consequently, of all the joyous occasions of Judaism, the heartiest *Mazal Tov* is reserved for the wedding.

A. FROM ENGAGEMENT TO MARRIAGE

A-1 The *mitzvah* of marriage

קִדּוּשִׁין It is a *mitzvah* for a Jew to marry[37] and to live together with his/her spouse in a manner worthy of the traditional Hebrew designation for marriage, *Kiddushin*—set apart for each other in a sanctified relationship.[38]

In Judaism the decision to marry implies a willingness to enter wholeheartedly into a sacred covenant with another person.[39]

A-2 Consulting the rabbi

The couple should call the rabbi before any definite plans are made and arrange a meeting in order to discuss the ceremony and the meaning of marriage in the Jewish tradition as well as the date and place for the ceremony. If one of the partners in the marriage is a stranger to the rabbi and the congregation, an opportunity should be found for that partner and his/her family to meet the rabbi and to attend a service in the synagogue. The better the rabbi knows the couple, the more meaningful and personal the wedding ceremony will be.

The content of the premarital consultations will vary with rabbi and couple, but the couple should take advantage of the rabbi's experience and consult not only about the details of the wedding ceremony, but about the meaning of a Jewish home, Jewish attitudes toward sex and parenthood, the place of the couple in the congregation, and whatever else might concern them as they approach their new status in life.

A-3 Civil requirements

Civil law requires a marriage license and usually a blood test before a marriage may take place. The marriage license should be brought to the rabbi before the wedding ceremony.[40]

A-4   The *mitzvah* of testing for genetic disease

It is a *mitzvah* for a couple to be tested for genetic diseases before marriage,[41] in keeping with the fundamental Jewish principle of the sanctity of life. In those rare cases where both bride and groom are found to be carriers, they should seek out the best medical advice and should also consult with their rabbi.

A-5   The *mitzvah* of blessing in the synagogue

It is a *mitzvah* for a bride and groom to be blessed in the synagogue either on the occasion of the public announcement of their engagement or on the Sabbath preceding their marriage.[42] This ceremony may take different forms, depending upon the practices of the congregation. The traditional ceremony, often referred to as an *Aufruf*, consists of the groom being called to the Torah. In many Reform congregations the couple (and possibly other members of the family) will be called up

עֲלִיָה

for an *aliyah* and/or the rabbi will offer a prayer for God's blessings on their marriage.

In order to involve the entire congregation (among whom there will be many who will not be guests at the wedding itself), the family of the bride or groom

עֹנֶג שַׁבָּת
קִדוּש

may wish to sponsor the *oneg Shabbat* or *kiddush* following the service.

A-6   The *mitzvah* of conjugal pleasure

It is a *mitzvah* for a man and a woman, joined together in *Kiddushin*, to take pleasure in sexual union[43] and thereby enrich and strengthen their marriage.

A-7   Equality in marriage

כְּתֻבָּה

Although the Bible and later rabbinic literature attempted to protect married women, especially through the device of the *ketubah* (traditional Aramaic marriage contract; see C-4), it is clear that Judaism, which developed in a patriarchal society, traditionally projected the husband as the dominant figure in marriage while the wife was often subject to severe disabilities and indignities.[44]

In the Reform Jewish view, *Kiddushin* establishes a bond of mutuality between a man and a woman. They are equal partners in the home, consecrated to one another (see C-3) unconditionally. Therefore, any aspect of a marriage or the preparations for a marriage which suggests the dominance or the diminution of one or the other partner should be recognized as such and avoided.

B. *PROHIBITIONS OF PARTNER AND DATE*

B-1   Prohibited marriages

Since biblical times the laws of consanguinity (blood relationship) and affinity have prohibited marriages between certain relatives. These laws derive from the Torah and were extended in the Talmud.[45] Reform Judaism retains these prohibitions, as does civil law generally.

B-2   Inappropriate dates

תִּשְׁעָה בְּאָב

יוֹם הַשּׁוֹאָה

Jewish tradition has set aside certain days and periods during which weddings may not be held, primarily Sabbaths and major festivals.[46] Most rabbis would also consider Tish'a Be-Av, Yom Ha-Shoah,[47] and certain mourning periods (see "Mourning," D-2) as times not suitable for the joy of a marriage ceremony.[48]

Because of these and other prohibitions and the variations of practice among rabbis, it is extremely important to choose the date of the wedding in consultation with the rabbi.

B-3   Waiting before remarriage

Jewish tradition prohibits the remarriage of a widow within ninety days of her husband's death and of a divorcee within ninety days of the divorce decree.[49] Where there is no possibility of the birth of a child conceived before the death or divorce, there is no basis in Reform Judaism for a difference in waiting period between men and women. Propriety and prudence would indicate the lapse of at least thirty days, and preferably longer, before any remarriage for bride or groom.

Tradition further prescribes that a widower wait for the passing of three festivals (Pesach, Shavuot, and Sukkot—a time lapse of at least seven months) before remarrrying. This would seem to be a good rule for all, but special circumstances must always be considered. The rabbi's counsel should be sought here.

B-4   Death in the family

If the death of a close relative of the bride or groom (particularly a parent, brother, or sister) occurs shortly before the scheduled marriage, the rabbi should be consulted as to the advisability of postponement.

C.   *THE MARRIAGE CEREMONY*

C-1   The place for a wedding

The most appropriate place for a Jewish marriage ceremony is in one of the sanctuaries of Judaism, the synagogue or the home.[50] The marriage ceremony, which is קִדּוּשִׁין   traditionally called *Kiddushin*—holiness—should take

קְדוּשָׁה place in an atmosphere of *kedushah*. When a hotel, restaurant, public hall, or club is the locale for the wedding reception, the synagogue or home should be used, if possible, for the religious ceremony.

There is a tendency to return to the old custom of holding marriage ceremonies under the open sky.[51] But whatever location is chosen, the guiding principle is that the wedding be held in an atmosphere of *kedushah*.

C-2 Contents of the ceremony

The essential features of a Jewish marriage ceremony are the declarations made to each other by bride and groom, the sharing of wine, the giving or exchange of a ring or rings, and the recital of traditional blessings.[52]

Generally, the marriage ceremony will also include some or all of the following:[53] a marriage canopy חֻפָּה (*chuppah*),[54] escorts for the groom and the bride (*unter-* כְּתֻבָּה *führer*),[55] the reading of a *ketubah* (see C-4), and the breaking of a glass.[56]

Certain features of a wedding, e.g., the procession, the attendants, the degree of formality, etc., are matters of custom and etiquette which vary from family to family and from community to community.

The bride and groom should discuss the ceremony with the rabbi during the premarital interview so that there is a clear understanding of what will and will not be included and of the meaning of the content of the ceremony. The couple might want to include material particularly meaningful to them. This, too, should be discussed with the rabbi.

C-3 The vows and rings

Since the Reform wedding ceremony is one of equivalence between bride and groom, the vows should be recited by both. Tradition prescribes that the groom recite the following words as he places the ring on the finger of the bride: "*Harei at mekudeshet li be-tabaat zo ke-dat Mosheh ve-Yisrael*—Behold, you are consecrated to me by this ring according to the tradition of Moses and Israel."[57]

Whether or not the bride presents a ring to the groom, she should recite one of the following vows: "*Harei attah mekudash li (be-tabaat zo) ke-dat Mosheh ve-Yisrael*" (same translation as above, including or omitting "by this ring") or "*Ani le-dodi ve-dodi li*—I am my beloved's and my beloved is mine" (Song of Songs 6:3).

The ring or rings used may be plain or ornate.[58]

C-4   The marriage document or *ketubah*

A document, signed and witnessed,[59] attesting to the fact that a marriage ceremony has taken place will be prepared by the rabbi and given to the couple.

כְּתֻבָּה   Tradition requires the use of an Aramaic[60] legal document called a *ketubah*, which specifies the financial settlement to the bride in the event of a divorce or the death of the groom and the groom's obligation to support and maintain the bride. There are many modern variations of the *ketubah*, some of them beautifully worded and illuminated, which emphasize the mutual spiritual obligations of bride and groom while omitting finances and legalisms. The couple might want to discuss the advisability of using a *ketubah*, or some variant of it, with the rabbi.

C-5   *Kedushah* and dignity

As with all other aspects of a Jewish wedding, a sense קְדוּשָׁה   of *kedushah* and dignity should govern the choice of music. Jewish wedding music is readily available and should be selected in consultation with the rabbi, cantor, or music director of the congregation.

The same sense of *kedushah* and good taste should

govern the overall decorum of the wedding ceremony and the subsequent reception. Cocktail receptions preceding the ceremony should be avoided. Photographs should not be taken during the ceremony, nor should anything else be done which might detract from the solemnity of the occasion.

C-6   Expenses

A sense of dignity and proportion should govern the expenditures connected with weddings and especially wedding receptions. As with all life-cycle ceremonies, lavish display is destructive of the atmosphere of *kedushah* which should be present when a new family is established in the Jewish people.

C-7   The *mitzvah* of *tzedakah*

צְדָקָה   It is a *mitzvah* to make a gift of *tzedakah* in honor of one's marriage or in honor of the marriage of one's children.[61]

D.   DIVORCE, REMARRIAGE, AND MIXED MARRIAGE

D-1   Divorce

Judaism has allowed divorce since earliest times,[62] often on quite liberal grounds. However, the sanctity of home and family being cardinal principles of Judaism, divorce in the Jewish community was relatively rare and was usually considered a misfortune.[63]

Today the family is subjected to pressures unparalleled in history, and, consequently, divorce is on the increase in both the Jewish and non-Jewish communities. Couples experiencing difficulty in their marriages should seek out the rabbi, who will counsel with them and possibly direct them to a professional counsellor to help them through their difficulties. A frank reappraisal of the strengths and weaknesses of a marriage under professional guidance will often bring together alienated people and reestablish a marriage on more solid, possibly more sacred, foundations.

D-2   The *get*

גֵּט   While traditional Judaism requires the obtaining of a religious divorce decree (a *get*) before a divorced person may remarry,[64] Reform rabbis will generally accept a civil divorce as sufficient. The decision as to whether or not it is advisable to obtain a *get* before remarriage should be made in consultation with the rabbi.

Lawyers should familiarize themselves with the procedures related to obtaining a *get* in order to advise their clients more fully.

D-3   Remarriage

Judaism, consonant with its emphasis on life, urges remarriage as preferable to living alone (see B-3 and "Death and Mourning," D-12).

If there are children from a previous marriage, their feelings should be carefully considered in the planning of a remarriage. If possible, they should be in attendance at the wedding ceremony and may be included in the bridal party.

D-4   The *mitzvah* of marriage within Judaism

It is a *mitzvah* for a Jew to marry a Jew so that the sacred heritage of Judaism may be transmitted most effectively from generation to generation.[65]

As might be expected, though, in an open society, marriage between Jews and non-Jews is increasing. The problem is a serious one, and therefore any Jew who is considering marriage to a non-Jew should consult with his/her rabbi.

מִקְדָּשׁ מְעַט

Judaism resists mixed marriages[66] because it weakens the fabric of family relationship and the survival potential of the Jewish community, and because it makes it more difficult to establish the *mikdash me-at* (see E-1 below) that should be the goal of every Jewish marriage. The crucial question of Jewish survival is especially compelling in this post-Holocaust era.

E. *ESTABLISHING A JEWISH HOME*

E-1 The *mitzvah* of sanctifying the home

מִקְדָּשׁ מְעַט

It is a *mitzvah* to establish a home which is worthy of the designation *mikdash me-at*—a miniature sanctuary (Ezekiel 11:16). It is the Jewish home, along with the synagogue, that has preserved the traditions and values of Judaism through centuries of dispersion.[67]

E-2 Home rituals

בְּרָכוֹת

קִדּוּשׁ

זְמִירוֹת

הַבְדָּלָה

סֵדֶר

סֻכָּה

In Judaism home-centered rituals and ceremonies are as important as those that are synagogue-centered. *Berachot* (blessings) over food, Shabbat and festival candles, *Kiddush* and *zemirot* (table songs), *Havdalah*, the Passover *Seder*, Chanukah lights, building a *sukkah*—these are but a few of the *mitzvot* which add to the sanctity of the Jewish home and family.

Prayers and services for these home ceremonies may be found in *Gates of the House, Gates of Prayer, A*

Shabbat Manual, and many other books that may be suggested by the rabbi (see "A Basic Library," page 133.)

E-3   *The mitzvah* of home prayer

It is a *mitzvah* to set aside a time for daily prayer. In many communities there are daily services in the synagogue, but prayer in the home is equally important and will have a profound influence on the individual and family.[68]

Daily services may be found in *Gates of Prayer* and *Gates of the House.* One may add to these such personal prayers as the heart and circumstances might prompt.

After rising in the morning and before retiring at night are particularly appropriate times for private or family prayer.[69]

E-4   The *mitzvah* of *mezuzah*

מְזוּזָה

שְׁמַע יִשְׂרָאֵל

It is a *mitzvah* to affix a *mezuzah* to the doorpost of a Jewish home.[70] The *mezuzah* is a small parchment scroll, usually inserted into a tubular case, upon which is written the *Shema Yisrael* and two passages from the Torah (Deuteronomy 6:4–9 and 11:13–21) that speak of the love due to God and His teachings. Some follow the tradition of affixing a *mezuzah* not only to the main-entry doorpost but to the doorposts of each major room in the house.

חֲנֻכַּת הַבַּיִת

The *mezuzah* should be fastened to the upper part of the right doorpost (as one enters) in a diagonal position (the top part inward)[71] so that it may be seen easily on entering or leaving the home. One may affix the *mezuzah* privately or invite friends and family for a *Chanukat ha-Bayit* (dedication of a home) ceremony.

The following blessing is recited as the *mezuzah* is attached:

בָּרוּךְ אַתָּה, יְיָ אֱלֹהֵינוּ, מֶלֶךְ הָעוֹלָם,
אֲשֶׁר קִדְּשָׁנוּ בְּמִצְוֹתָיו
וְצִוָּנוּ לִקְבּוֹעַ מְזוּזָה.

**Ba-ruch a-ta, A-do-nai E-lo-hei-nu, me-lech ha-o-lam,
asher ki-de-sha-nu be-mits-vo-tav
ve-tsi-va-nu lik-bo-a me-zu-zah.**

*Blessed is the Lord our God, Ruler of the universe,
by whose* mitzvot *we are hallowed, who commands
us to affix the* mezuzah.

A complete service for the dedication of a home may be found in *Gates of the House,* pages 103–7.

The *mezuzah* is not a good luck charm.[72] It is, rather, a symbolic acknowledgment that God is a partner in the home: "Unless the Lord builds the house, its builders labor in vain" (Psalms 127:1).

E-5 Contents of the Jewish home

תַּלְמוּד תּוֹרָה In keeping with the *mitzvah* of *Talmud Torah* (see "Birth, Childhood, and Education," F-1 and F-3), a Jewish home should have a library, and time should be set aside for the study of Torah.[73] We are taught to "meditate on it [the Torah] day and night" (Joshua 1:8 and Psalms 1:2), that we should "teach it diligently" to our children, and that we should discuss it in our homes (Deuteronomy 6:7). (See "A Basic Library," page 133.)

Other items which should be conspicuously present and used in a Jewish home are: Shabbat and festival candlesticks, a *Kiddush* goblet, a *Seder* plate, and a

צְדָקָה   *tzedakah* box. As there should be regular periods for prayer and sacred study in a Jewish home, there should also be regular times for putting money into the *tzedakah* box. The final moments before kindling the Shabbat candles each week might be a good opportunity for the *mitzvah* of *tzedakah*.

E-6   The tradition of *kashrut*

בַּשְׁרוּת   Many Reform Jews observe certain traditional dietary disciplines as a part of their attempt to establish a Jewish home and life style. For some, traditional *kashrut* will enhance the sanctity of the home and be observed as a *mitzvah;* for some, a degree of *kashrut* (e.g., the avoidance of pork products and/or shellfish) may be meaningful; and still others may find nothing of value in *kashrut* (see the essay on *kashrut*, page 130). However, the fact that *kashrut* was an essential feature of Jewish life for so many centuries should motivate the Jewish family to study it and to consider whether or not it may enhance the sanctity of their home.

E-7   The *mitzvah* of table blessings

הַמּוֹצִיא   It is a *mitzvah* to treat the daily family mealtime as a sacred event, beginning with the recitation of the prayer known as *Ha-Motsi:*

בָּרוּךְ אַתָּה, יְיָ אֱלֹהֵינוּ, מֶלֶךְ הָעוֹלָם,
הַמּוֹצִיא לֶחֶם מִן־הָאָרֶץ.

Ba-ruch a-ta, A-do-nai E-lo-hei-nu, me-lech ha-o-lam, ha-mo-tsi le-chem min ha-a-rets.

Blessed is the Lord our God, Ruler of the universe, who causes bread to come forth from the earth.

בִּרְכַּת הַמָּזוֹן Traditionally the meal concludes with a prayer of thanks, *Birkat Ha-Mazon*,[74] which may be found in *Gates of the House*, pages 6–18. If the family cannot recite *Birkat Ha-Mazon* daily, they should do so at least after Shabbat dinner.

מִקְדָּשׁ מְעַט
מִזְבֵּחַ As it is the ideal of the Jewish family to make its home into a *mikdash me-at* (see E-1), the table should be considered a *mizbei-ach*—an altar.[75] The family mealtime is an excellent opportunity for the discussion of matters that transcend the trivial. A daily family dinner hour that transforms the table into an altar will strengthen both the family and the Jewish people.

E-8 The *mitzvah* of the Shabbat table

חַלָּה It is a *mitzvah* for the family to gather together and consecrate the Shabbat and festival table with candles, *Kiddush* wine, and *challah*, and to recite the appropriate blessings.[76]

If the Jewish home is a miniature sanctuary during the ordinary days of the week, how much more so on Shabbat and festivals. Shabbat and festival dinner hours should be prolonged and should include *zemirot* (table songs), study and discussion (the Torah portion of the week is particularly appropriate), and *Birkat Ha-Mazon*. Songs and services may be found in *A Shabbat Manual* and in *Gates of the House*, pages 29–40.

E-9 The *mitzvah* of blessing children

It is a *mitzvah* for parents to bless their children at the Shabbat table each week.[77] Families may establish their own ritual of blessing or may use the traditional words:

FOR A BOY

יְשִׂמְךָ אֱלֹהִים כְּאֶפְרַיִם וְכִמְנַשֶּׁה.

Ye-sim-cha E-lo-him ke-Ef-ra-im ve-chi-Me-na-sheh.

May God inspire you to live in the tradition of Ephraim and Menasheh, who carried forward the life of our people.

FOR A GIRL

יְשִׂמֵךְ אֱלֹהִים כְּשָׂרָה, רִבְקָה,
רָחֵל, וְלֵאָה.

**Ye-si-meich E-lo-him ke-Sa-ra, Riv-ka,
Ra-cheil, ve-Lei-a.**

May God inspire you to live in the tradition of Sarah and Rebekah, Rachel and Leah, who carried forward the life of our people.

יְבָרֶכְךָ יְיָ וְיִשְׁמְרֶךָ,
יָאֵר יְיָ פָּנָיו אֵלֶיךָ וִיחֻנֶּךָּ,
יִשָּׂא יְיָ פָּנָיו אֵלֶיךָ וְיָשֵׂם לְךָ שָׁלוֹם.
אָמֵן.

**Ye-va-re-che-cha A-do-nai ve-yish-me-re-cha;
Ya-eir A-do-nai pa-nav ei-le-cha vi-chu-ne-ka;
Yi-sa A-do-nai pa-nav ei-le-cha ve-ya-seim le-cha shalom.
A-mein.**

*The Lord bless you and keep you;
The Lord look kindly upon you and be gracious to you;
The Lord bestow His favor upon you and give you peace.
Amen.*[78]

E-10   The *mitzvah* of hospitality

It is a *mitzvah* to have guests at one's table, especially for the celebration of Shabbat and festivals. One should pay particular attention to strangers and others who do not have families of their own. This *mitzvah* is called הַכְנָסַת אוֹרְחִים *hachnasat orchim*, and Jewish tradition includes it among those which merit eternal reward.[79]

E-11   Joyous family occasions

Joyous family occasions, such as birthdays, anniversaries, the birth of children and grandchildren, marriages, and academic and career achievements, should be marked by prayers of gratitude. Several suggested prayers may be found in *Gates of the House*, pages 94–124, or one may offer a personal prayer.

The traditional prayer for all occasions of joy is:

בָּרוּךְ אַתָּה, יְיָ אֱלֹהֵינוּ, מֶלֶךְ הָעוֹלָם,
שֶׁהֶחֱיָנוּ וְקִיְּמָנוּ וְהִגִּיעָנוּ
לַזְּמַן הַזֶּה.

Ba-ruch a-ta, A-do-nai E-lo-hei-nu, me-lech ha-o-lam, she-he-che-ya-nu ve-ki-ye-ma-nu ve-hi-gi-a-nu la-ze-man ha-zeh.

Blessed is the Lord our God, Ruler of the universe, for giving us life, for sustaining us, and for enabling us to reach this joyous occasion.

E-12   The *mitzvah* of joining a congregation

It is a *mitzvah* for each Jew and each Jewish family to join a synagogue and to make use of its facilities for prayer, Jewish education, and communal activities.[80]

בֵּית תְּפִלָּה
בֵּית מִדְרָשׁ
בֵּית כְּנֶסֶת
בֵּית עָם

It is the synagogue which, in partnership with the home (see E-1 above), has preserved the Jewish people, providing it with a center for prayer (*beit tefillah*), for study (*beit midrash*), and for assembly (*beit kenesset* or *beit am*). While prayer and study in the home are not only praiseworthy but are *mitzvot* of great importance, the synagogue is the communal center for these activities and, as such, should be attended regularly and supported generously.

It should be understood that in Reform Judaism women take part in the life of the synagogue equally with men. There is no religious function which may not be performed by a woman.

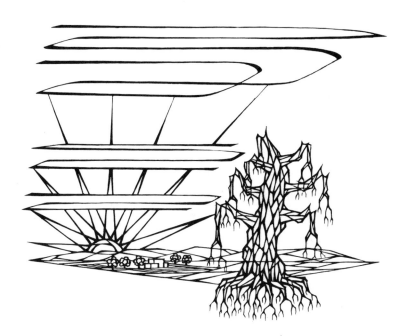

DEATH
and MOURNING

Though I walk through the valley
of the shadow of death,
I shall fear no evil,
for You are with me.

—PSALMS 23:4

They are like grass that renews itself;
In the morning it flourishes anew;
In the evening it withers and dries up. . . .
Teach us to count our days rightly,
That we may obtain a wise heart.

—PSALMS 90:5–6, 12

Naked I came from my mother's womb,
And naked shall I return there.
The Lord gave and the Lord took away;
Blessed be the name of the Lord.

—JOB 1:21

"J UDAISM teaches us to understand death as part of the Divine pattern of the universe. . . . Mortality is the tax we pay for the privilege of love, thought and creative work."[81] Thus, while Judaism has accumulated numerous *mitzvot* and customs relating to death and mourning, it has never sought to make a fetish of grief. Jewish tradition encourages a realistic acceptance of the inevitability of death and teaches the sacredness of grief, sympathy, and memory.

The *mitzvot* related to death and mourning are governed by certain principles, the first of these being moderation in grief. Tradition established the various periods of mourning in order to allow and, indeed, encourage the pouring out of one's grief. But these periods were established also to *limit* mourning, so that people might return to their normal pursuits without having to fear the disapproval of the community. There is always the danger that the bereaved, for whatever reasons, might indulge in elaborate, painful, and lengthy periods of mourning, but on this the tradition speaks out clearly: "We must not mourn for the dead excessively."[82]

A closely related second principle is the recognition of the reality of death.[83] Tradition prescribes certain conduct at the bedside of a dying person, in the preparation of the body for burial, at the funeral, and in the house of mourning that should help mourners to accept their loss and express their grief, so that the pain might be eased gradually and the mourners make a healthy adjustment.

A third basic principle is respect for the dead. Since biblical times Judaism has established the principle that every dead person, even the basest criminal, must be accorded the honor of proper burial (Deuteronomy 21:22–23). If there was no family, the *mitzvah* was incumbent upon the Jewish community, every member of which was expected to assist at the burial of the dead[84] and the comforting of mourners.

And the fourth principle is equality in death; "the small and great are there alike, and the servant is free of his master" (Job 3:19). Time and again in the traditional texts of Judaism we see evidence of the sensitivity of the Rabbis toward the poor, but nowhere is this more marked than in the meticulously spelled out funeral procedures, where we find a deep compassion for the mourners as well as an understanding of their vulnerability.[85]

It is in the spirit of these time-hallowed principles that we now proceed to a detailed consideration of the *mitzvot* and customs of death and mourning in Judaism.

A. THE APPROACH OF DEATH

A-1 The *mitzvah* of prayer for the sick

It is a *mitzvah* to offer prayers in private or in the synagogue for the seriously ill. Appropriate prayers may be found in *Gates of the House* (pages 125–28) and in the Psalms (especially Psalms 6, 23, 88, 121, and 130). The custom of praying for the ill in the synagogue varies from congregation to congregation. One should inform the rabbi and consult with him in cases of serious illness.

A-2 Medical care

While Judaism prescribes prayer by and for the sick, it never prescribes prayer as a substitute for competent medical treatment. Prayer directs one's heart to God, who is ultimately the source of healing, as we read: "My cure comes from God, the Creator of physicians."[86]

A-3 The *mitzvah* of *bikkur cholim*

בְּקוּר חוֹלִים

It is a *mitzvah* to visit the sick. Jewish tradition considers *bikkur cholim*—the visiting of the sick—to be a basic commandment and suggests that the person who performs this *mitzvah* will achieve eternal reward.[87] The object of *bikkur cholim* is to relieve the isolation of the sick, to cheer them, to be of service, and to give them hope.[88]

A-4 The *mitzvah* of offering thanks

It is a *mitzvah* to offer a prayer of thanks, either privately or in the synagogue, when one recovers from a serious illness. The following is the traditional prayer on recovering from illness:

בָּרוּךְ אַתָּה, יְיָ אֱלֹהֵינוּ, מֶלֶךְ הָעוֹלָם,
שֶׁגְּמָלַנִי כָּל־טוֹב.

**Ba-ruch a-ta, A-do-nai E-lo-hei-nu, me-lech ha-o-lam,
she-ge-ma-la-ni kol tov.**

*Blessed is the Lord our God, Ruler of the universe,
who bestows great goodness upon me.*

Other prayers to be recited in illness or on recovery may
be found in *Gates of the House* (pages 125–27).

A-5　The *mitzvah* of *Viddui*

וִדּוּי

It is a *mitzvah* for a critically ill person to recite a special
prayer, *Viddui* (Confession), and it is equally a *mitzvah*
to help a person who has requested such help to recite it.
A prayer for the critically ill may be found in *Gates of
the House* (page 128).[89]

The customs of changing the name of a critically ill
person or of adding an extra name are discouraged in
Reform Judaism. These customs are of superstitious
origin and do not help patient or family to face the
reality of the situation.

A-6　Euthanasia

Judaism forbids euthanasia (i.e. *active* euthanasia, the
hastening of death); one must not do anything to hasten
the death of the terminally ill.[90] However, many of the
classic texts of Judaism assert with equal authority that
neither should one hinder the departure of the soul (i.e.,
passive euthanasia). "Heroic measures" to keep a person
alive through artificial systems of life support are, therefore, not required.[91]

Where special letters of instruction have been left by the dying, the family should consult with the rabbi.

A-7   The *mitzvah* of writing an ethical will

צַוָּאָה   It is a *mitzvah* to prepare an ethical will—a *tzavaah*—for the moral edification of the family, particularly the children.[92]

It is advisable to prepare such a will (as one would prepare a legal will) when one is in good health and strength. (For examples of notable ethical wills, see the Appendix, page 139)

B.   FROM DEATH TO FUNERAL

B-1   The *mitzvah* of *Tzidduk Ha-Din*

It is a *mitzvah* for members of the immediate family (i.e., children, parents, spouses, and siblings), when informed of a death, to recite the prayer:

בָּרוּךְ אַתָּה, יְיָ אֱלֹהֵינוּ, מֶלֶךְ הָעוֹלָם,
דַּיַּן הָאֱמֶת.

Ba-ruch a-ta, A-do-nai E-lo-hei-nu, me-lech ha-o-lam, Da-yan ha-emet.

Blessed is the Lord our God, Ruler of the Universe, the righteous Judge.[93]

צְדוּק הַדִּין   This traditional prayer is called *Tzidduk Ha-Din*[94]—the justification of the decree—and is an affirmation of one's faith in God and of the acceptance of the inevitability of death, even in a moment of grievous loss.

B-2 Informing the rabbi

> As soon as death occurs, the rabbi should be informed and consulted.

B-3 Funeral preparations

> One should purchase burial plots and make known one's wishes about funeral and burial *before* the time of need. Much anguish and confusion can be avoided when the survivors have a clear idea of the wishes of the deceased. But one should not normally make specific funeral arrangements for a dying person until death has actually occurred.
>
> However, in cases where the deceased leaves unusual instructions (e.g., that there be no funeral or that something other than a conventional religious service be held), the sensitivities of the survivors may be taken into consideration. In a case where the deceased leaves instructions contrary to the Jewish tradition, the rabbi should be consulted.

B-4 The *mitzvah* of donating organs

פְּקוּחַ נֶפֶשׁ

> It is a *mitzvah* to save a life and a *mitzvah* to heal the sick. According to Jewish tradition, *pikuach nefesh*—the saving of life—takes precedence over everything.[95] Therefore, Reform Judaism approves the donation of the organs of one's body for the purpose of transplantation in order to save a life or to heal a deficiency.

B-5 Autopsies and donating the body to science

> Autopsies are permitted in Reform Judaism[96] and are, in fact, recommended as long as they are performed for the clear purpose of increasing medical knowledge. If the dead person has left negative instructions as to autopsy, these instructions should be honored except where there

is the danger of epidemic or where civil law requires it.

While Jewish tradition forbids the donating of one's entire body to science, Reform Judaism permits this practice provided that the scientific institution to which the body is donated is known to treat the body with respect and that, when the study is completed, the remains are buried or cremated (see also C-11 and C-19).[97]

B-6 The *mitzvah* of notifying the family

It is a *mitzvah* to notify all members of the family at the time of a death. This applies also to cases where certatin members of the family are estranged and the period of family mourning might promote reconciliation.

B-7 Preparation of the body

טָהֳרָה

חֶבְרָה קַדִּישָׁא

There are many complex ancient and medieval traditions connected with the cleansing and preparation of the dead body (i.e., *taharah*). These may or may not be observed by Reform Jews. The body should be released by the family to any reputable funeral director or *Chevrah Kadisha* (Jewish communal burial society) with the simple instruction that it be prepared for burial.

Since Judaism prescribes that the body should be returned to the dust from which it came, embalming is discouraged except when required by law or circumstances.

B-8 Clothing for the dead

תַּכְרִיכִים

טַלִּית

The dead may be buried in ordinary clothing or in shrouds. *Tachrichim* (traditional linen burial shrouds) may be used but are not required. If the deceased directed that he be buried with his *tallit* (prayer shawl) or with a pouch of earth from the land of Israel, these directions should be honored.

B-9   Closing the coffin

The body, after having been prepared for burial, should be put into the coffin and the coffin closed. Jewish tradition is opposed to the public viewing of the deceased in an open coffin. The family may view the body privately before the funeral service if they wish, but the coffin should be permanently sealed before the service begins.[98]

The custom of pre-funeral visitation in the chapel is not in keeping with Jewish tradition and is discouraged.

B-10   *Keriah*

קְרִיעָה   *Keriah*, the rending of one's garment or the symbolic cutting of a black ribbon, is left to the discretion of the rabbi and the family.[99]

B-11   The *mitzvah* of helping the bereaved

It is a *mitzvah* to help the bereaved through the many difficult details of funeral arrangement. Recognizing the emotional vulnerability of mourners in these most painful hours of grief (i.e., the hours between death and burial), relatives and close friends should offer whatever help they can, but this is not a time for ordinary condolence calls.

C.   *THE FUNERAL SERVICE AND BURIAL*

C-1   The *mitzvah* of burying the dead

It is a *mitzvah* to bury the dead with all due respect. The Rabbis taught that there are ten *mitzvot* for which a person would enjoy eternal reward;[100] among these is attending to the dead (see C-9).

C-2 Responsibility for burial

The *mitzvah* of burying the dead is the responsibility of a person's children or spouse.[101] In cases where there are no children or spouse, it is the responsibility of the nearest relative. Where there is no family, the *mitzvah* should be assumed by the entire Jewish community.[102]

C-3 Timely burial

Funeral services and burial should not be delayed needlessly. Tradition teaches that we should bury within a day after death.[103] For us today the principle is to conduct the funeral and burial as soon as is practical but without undue haste (this generally means within two days of death). The rabbi should be informed as soon as death occurs and should be consulted about the time of the service.

C-4 Sabbaths and festivals

Funeral services are not held on Sabbaths and major festivals.[104] The rabbi should be consulted about burial on the second day of a festival.[105]

C-5 Simplicity and dignity

Simplicity and dignity are the governing principles for funeral arrangements. A funeral should never become an occasion for display.[106] It is preferable to use a simple wooden coffin, but in any case, the principle of simplicity should be honored. The same principle applies to the use of flowers.

C-6 The *mitzvah* of *tzedakah*

צְדָקָה It is a *mitzvah* to express sympathy by making a gift of *tzedakah* in memory of the deceased. Many families include a request to send contributions to charity (e.g., "in lieu of flowers") in the obituary notice.

C-7   Participation in the service

> If the family of the deceased desire the participation of
> any other person or any organization at the funeral serv-
> ice in addition to the rabbi, the rabbi should be con-
> sulted before an invitation is extended. The funeral
> service should always be arranged in consultation with
> the rabbi.

C-8   The *mitzvah* of eulogy

הֶסְפֵּד
> It is a *mitzvah* to speak well of the dead.[107] A funeral
> sermon or eulogy (*hesped*) is not required but is in-
> cluded at the discretion of the rabbi and family. There
> are no restrictions in Reform Judaism as to the days on
> which eulogies may be given.[108]

C-9   The *mitzvah* of attending a funeral

הַלְוָיַת הַמֵּת
> It is a *mitzvah* for all who are able to do so to attend a
> funeral service. This *mitzvah* is referred to as *halvayat
> ha-met.*[109] Those who can should also accompany the
> body to the cemetery unless the family has requested
> privacy for the interment.

C-10   Places for funerals

> The proper places for funeral services are the home of
> the deceased, the graveside, a funeral home, a cemetery
> chapel, or, in cases where the practice is allowed, the
> synagogue.

C-11   Burial, cremation, and entombment

> Burial is the most widely practiced method of disposi-
> tion of the body among Jews and is, in fact, the only
> method allowed by tradition.[110] However, it is clear
> that other methods (e.g., interment in caves) were prac-
> ticed among Jews in ancient times. And so, while both

cremation and entombment in mausoleums are acceptable in Reform Judaism, burial is the normative Jewish practice.

The Jewish dead should, if possible, be interred in Jewish cemeteries or in the Jewish sections of community cemeteries or mausoleums. In cases of cremation, the ashes should be buried in a Jewish cemetery or on one's private property or placed in the niche of a Jewish mausoleum.[111]

C-12 Burial of non-Jews

Reform Judaism permits non-Jewish members of Jewish families to be interred in Jewish cemeteries or mausoleums, provided that non-Jewish services are not recited and non-Jewish symbols are not displayed.[112]

C-13 Kaddish at graveside

מִנְיָן

קַדִּישׁ

Reform Judaism does not require the presence of a minyan[113] for the recitation of Kaddish[114] at the graveside. This Kaddish should be recited by the children, spouse, siblings, and parents of the deceased. Relatives and friends may join the mourners in the Kaddish. If the deceased was not survived by any of the above, the Kaddish should be recited by the closest relative or friend present or by the rabbi.

C-14 Filling the grave

Jewish tradition prescribes that the family of the deceased remain at the graveside for the lowering of the coffin and the refilling of the grave. In cases where the family chooses not to remain through the completion of the burial, a representative of the family should remain until the coffin is covered with earth. Some follow the custom that those present assist in the filling of the grave.

C-15 Burial vaults

Jewish tradition does not prescribe the use of a burial vault, but where state law or cemetery regulations require it, it is acceptable.

C-16 Children at funerals

Children should not be excluded from attendance at family funerals. In cases of doubt, the rabbi should be consulted. Children's questions about death, funeral, and burial should be answered, and they should be helped in every way to accept the reality of death.

C-17 No one excluded

It is a *mitzvah* to conduct a regular funeral service for all Jews, regardless of the style of their lives or the manner of their death.[115] All should be treated with the respect due every member of the Jewish community and should be buried in the Jewish cemetery in the midst of their families.

C-18 Non-viable infants

Tradition provides that funeral and mourning customs not be observed for the stillborn child or for an infant that does not live for thirty days. However, any infant who survives birth may be buried with a simple graveside service. In such a case the rabbi should be consulted.

C-19 Donated or unrecovered bodies

The regular funeral service should be conducted in the synagogue or the home for those whose bodies have been donated to science and for those whose bodies have been lost or cannot be recovered or identified.[116] For the latter, the service should be held and the period of mourning begin as soon as it becomes clear that there is no hope of recovering the body.[117]

D. *THE MOURNING PERIOD*

D-1 The *mitzvah* of mourning

It is a *mitzvah* to mourn for one's dead.[118] Grief, however, is a very personal emotion; it cannot be legislated. The Talmud, even as it established the laws of mourning, recognized that there is a difference between formal rites of mourning and private grief, "for grief is borne in the heart alone."[119]

D-2 Traditional mourning periods

Jewish tradition prescribes several periods of mourning, differing in intensity and obligation, following the death of a loved one. These are:

אֲבֵלוֹת   *Aveilut*—this is the name applied generally to the entire mourning period.

אֲנִינוּת   *Aninut*—the period between death and burial. During this period tradition prescribes that the mourner be free from all ritual and social obligations except the observance of the Sabbath (if it occurs) and the arrangement of the funeral and burial.[120]

שִׁבְעָה   *Shivah*—the seven days of mourning following the funeral. Mourners are encouraged to remain at home during these days (except on Shabbat or festivals, when they should join the congregation in prayer), to refrain from their ordinary pursuits and occupations, and to participate in daily services in the home. (Home services for *shivah* may be found in *Gates of the House*, pages 131–208.) The first three days of the *shivah* period are considered the most intense[121] and in Reform congregations are considered the minimum mourning period.

שְׁלֹשִׁים   *Sheloshim*—the thirty-day period (including *shivah*) when normal life gradually resumes and the mourners return to their daily activities while yet observing certain aspects of mourning. One should avoid joyful social events and entertainment during this period. This is the traditionally prescribed period of mourning for relatives other than parents.

The First Year—the period during which a mourner קַדִּישׁ recites *Kaddish* for a parent (see D-7 and D-8).

D-3   Intervention of Shabbat and festivals

Formal mourning (i.e., the observance of *shivah*) is suspended for the observance of Shabbat and festivals, at which times the mourners should attend synagogue services and observe the customs of the day.

Tradition prescribes the complete termination of *shivah* when a festival intervenes, but while Reform Judaism agrees to the suspension of formal mourning for the holy day itself, it is left to the family to decide whether or not to resume *shivah* after a festival, particularly when the festival falls within a day or two of the death. If death occurs during the intermediate days of a festival חוֹל הַמּוֹעֵד (i.e., *chol ha-mo-eid* Pesach or Sukkot), the rabbi should be consulted about the mourning period.[122]

D-4   The *mitzvah* of comforting the mourners

It is a *mitzvah* to go to a house of mourning to comfort the mourners there and to join them in study and prayer; נְחוּם אֲבֵלִים this *mitzvah* is called *nichum avelim* (comforting the mourners). When performing the *mitzvah* of *nichum avelim,* one should refrain from frivolous or lighthearted conversation. The days of *shivah* are consecrated to the memory of the deceased, and it is, therefore, a *mitzvah* to speak well of them to the mourners and to do acts צְדָקָה of *tzedakah* in their memory.[123]

דְּבַר תּוֹרָה   It is appropriate to include a *devar Torah* (a brief Torah lesson) in *shivah* services.[124]

D-5 The *mitzvah* of the first meal

סְעֻדַּת הַבְרָאָה

It is a *mitzvah* for friends to prepare the first meal eaten by the mourners on returning from the cemetery in order to spare the mourners the need of preparing food at the height of their grief. This meal of consolation (traditionally known as *se-udat havraah*)[125] should not become an occasion for lavish feasting and drinking; it should, rather, be a time for family and close friends to come together to lend their strength to the bereaved. The practice of serving refreshments to visitors during *shivah* is discouraged.

D-6 The *shivah* candle

It is customary to light a seven-day candle on returning from the cemetery as a memorial to the deceased, symbolic of the light brought by the deceased to the mourners during life.[126] (A brief service may be found in *Gates of the House,* page 130.) This candle should be put in a conspicuous place so that it may be seen, especially during *shivah* services. The candle should be lit by one of the mourners. As it is lit, the family says:

נֵר יְיָ נִשְׁמַת אָדָם.
בָּרוּךְ אַתָּה, יְיָ,
נוֹטֵעַ בְּתוֹכֵנוּ חַיֵּי עוֹלָם.

Neir A-do-nai nish-mat a-dam.
Ba-ruch a-ta, A-do-nai,
no-tei-a be-to-chei-nu cha-yei o-lam.

The human spirit is the lamp of God.
Blessed is the Eternal One, who has implanted
within us eternal life.

D-7   The *mitzvah* of *Kaddish*

קַדִּישׁ   It is a *mitzvah* for mourners to recite the *Kaddish* prayer in memory of the dead at daily services during *shivah* at home and thereafter in the synagogue.[127] If there is no daily service in the synagogue, mourners should recite *Kaddish* with their families or privately.[128] In addition to *Kaddish,* one or more of the following appropriate psalms should be added to one's public or private prayers יָאר־צַיְט   during the week of *shivah* and on *yahrzeit* (see D-9): Psalms 15, 16, 23, 49, 90, and 121.

In Reform Judaism the *mitzvah* of *Kaddish* is incumbent on men and women equally.

D-8   The *mitzvah* of *Kaddish* for a year

It is a *mitzvah* to recite *Kaddish* for parents for a year[129] and for other members of the family for a month. As the memory of loved ones inspires the performance of such *mitzvot* as prayer, charity, and study, the dead are immortalized in the lives of those who remember them.

The *mitzvah* of *Kaddish* is incumbent on the mourners themselves. Reform Judaism does not consider the *mitzvah* fulfilled when the mourner engages someone else to attend services and recite *Kaddish* in his or her place. (cf. *Gates of the House*, p. 207.)

D-9   The *mitzvah* of *yahrzeit*

It is a *mitzvah* to observe the *yahrzeit* (the anniversary of the day of death) each year with the recitation of *Kaddish* and attendance at synagogue services.[130] It is customary to light a twenty-four-hour candle on the eve of the *yahrzeit* date. A home *yahrzeit* service may be found in *Gates of the House*, page 216.

A family may choose to observe either the Hebrew or the secular date of death, but whichever date is chosen should be agreed to by the entire family, so that all may observe the occasion at the same time and, if possible, together.

Yahrzeit is not an occasion for renewed mourning but rather a day consecrated each year to the memory of the dead. The observance of *yahrzeit* should move the family to the performance of *mitzvot* (e.g., *tzedakah* and study) in honor of the deceased.

D-10 The *mitzvah* of *Yizkor*

יִזְכּוֹר   It is a *mitzvah* to recite *Yizkor* and to devote a part of our festival prayers to the memories of the loved ones whose names we recall.[131] The recitation of *Yizkor* should be accompanied by the *mitzvah* of appropriate *tzedakah* in memory of the deceased.

D-11 Customs not observed

There are certain mourning practices and abstinences which have had wide currency among Jews through the centuries but which Reform Jews need not observe.[132] In cases of doubt, the rabbi should be consulted.

D-12 Remarriage

Judaism, consonant with its emphasis on life, prescribes remarriage as preferable to living alone, but remarriage is a personal decision which must be faced by a bereaved spouse, especially if the bereavement occurs early in life (see "Marriage and the Jewish Home," B-3 and D-3).

D-13 The *mitzvah* of a memorial marker

מַצֵּבָה   It is a *mitzvah* to set up a tombstone or memorial marker —a *matzevah*—in memory of the dead.[133] The same principles of simplicity and dignity that govern the choice of coffins (see C-5) should govern the choice of tombstones.

D-14   Dedicating a memorial

Tombstone dedications or unveilings are not required by Jewish tradition. However, it is praiseworthy for a family to go to the cemetery together at some time after the monument or marker is set in place for a consecration service. This service might best be held after *sheloshim* (see D-2) or on or before the date of the first *yahrzeit*. The consecration service may be read by members of the family. A suggested service for "Consecration of a Memorial" may be found in *Gates of the House,* pages 208–15.

D-15   Visiting graves

It is customary to visit the graves of loved ones before the High Holy Days. It is, however, inappropriate to visit graves on Sabbaths or festivals, when the prevailing mood should be *oneg* (pleasure) and *simchah* (joy).

עֹנֶג
שִׂמְחָה

D-16   The *mitzvah* of *tzedakah*

It is a *mitzvah* to establish an appropriate memorial to the deceased. Depending on its means, the family should establish such a memorial in the form of a significant act of *tzedakah*. It is best to consult with the rabbi about this.

NOTES

Sources and Elucidations

The notes that follow are very much a part of this book, and it is for this reason that they have been put here—directly following the three chapters on the *mitzvot* of the life cycle—rather than at the end of the book.

Some will use this book from time to time for the immediate and practical purpose of finding out what they, as Jews, should do to celebrate events in the life cycle of their families. It was for these people, in the first instance, that *Shaarei Mitzvah* was written. But others will want to use this book to deepen their knowledge of Judaism. For the latter it will not be enough to read that a Jew should do this or that; they will want to know why. What is the source of the *mitzvah*? How does Reform practice differ fom traditional practice and why? Where can one learn more about this?

It is these questions that are addressed in the notes that follow. In these pages the reader will find not only references to the classical sources but also elucidations: expansions and clarifications that may help the reader get to the *tamtzit*—the essential core—of the *mitzvah*.

Some of the sources cited and some of the Hebrew terms used here and elsewhere in *Shaarei Mitzvah* may not be familiar to the reader. This is the reason for the Glossary at the end of the Appendix. The Glossary explains all Hebrew terms found in this book, and is followed by a list of classic Jewish texts.

BIRTH AND CHILDHOOD

[1] The Talmud is quite specific in a number of instances about the responsibility of the community for the proper raising and educating of a child. Of course, the primary responsibility rests with the child's parents, but when there are no parents or when the parents are incapable, the responsibility rests with the Jewish community. The Talmud (*Baba Bathra* 21a) points out that there was a time when children without parents were not educated. How did the rabbis learn that it is a *mitzvah* for the community to educate such children? From the verse "And you shall teach them to your children" (Deuteronomy 11:19), laying the emphasis on the word "you" (plural). In the earlier, better-known passage in Deuteronomy, the text reads "and you [singular] shall teach them" (6:7). Thus, we learn that the primary responsibility rests on the parent and the secondary responsibility on the community.

[2] The Jewish doctrine of innate purity is a very ancient one, deriving from the concept of the human being having been created in the image of God. The doctrine is set forth explicitly in the Talmud and Midrash in many places, e.g., "As God is pure, so also the soul is pure" (*Berachot* 10a), "As the spirit was given to you pure, so return it pure" (*Shabbat* 152b), etc.

That this doctrine of innate purity is very much a part of Reform Jewish belief may be attested by the fact that the ancient talmudic prayer thanking God for the purity of the soul ("My God, the soul which You placed within me is pure. You fashioned it; You breathed it into me; You sustain it within me; and You will one day take it from me . . ." *Berachot* 60b) was preserved in the old *Union Prayer Book* (p. 101) and in *Gates of Prayer* (pp. 53 *et seq.*) as it is in all traditional Jewish prayerbooks.

[3] Maimonides lists "Be fruitful and multiply" among the 248 positive commandments in his *Sefer Ha-Mitzvot*. The *Shulchan Aruch* rules that the requirement of the *mitzvah* is fulfilled once a person has had both a son and a daughter (*Even Ha-Ezer* 1:5).

[4] A position paper on Jewish Family Planning, presented to the 1977 CCAR Convention by the Committee on Family Life, agrees sub-

stantially with A-2, but it adds: "We also recognize our obligation to maintain a viable and stable Jewish population. Therefore, couples are encouraged to have at least two or three children."

[5] Mishnah, *Oholot* 7:6. "If a woman is giving birth with great difficulty, the fetus can be dismembered within her and extracted limb by limb, because the life of the mother takes precedence over the life of the fetus . . ." For a complete study of Jewish tradition and law in the areas of birth control, abortion, etc., see David Feldman's *Birth Control in Jewish Law* (New York, 1968).

[6] Resolution of the CCAR, 1967 (*Yearbook*, vol. 77, p. 103). This resolution encourages the liberalization of abortion laws and recognizes that "the preservation of a mother's emotional health [is] as important as her physical well-being."

[7] Talmud B., *Sanhedrin* 19b. "Whoever raises an orphan in his home, Scripture considers him as if he were the natural parent."

[8] Procreation, in the traditional Jewish view, requires not only a man and a woman, but the presence of God as an equal creative partner. Thus, the act of procreation is sanctified and spiritualized. As the Midrash teaches: "Man [does not fulfil his destiny] without woman, nor woman without man, nor the two of them together without the Divine Presence" (*Genesis Rabbah* 8:9).

[9] See the essay on *tzedakah* in the Appendix, p. 121.

[10] Talmud B., *Gittin* 57a. "It was the custom when a boy was born to plant a cedar tree and when a girl was born to plant a pine tree, and when they married the tree was cut down and a canopy made of the branches."

[11] See Deuteronomy 29:9–14. The Midrash takes the poetic parallelism of Exodus 19:3 to prove that the revelation at Sinai and the consequent covenant were participated in equally by the men and the women of Israel. " 'Thus shall you say to the house of Jacob'—this refers to the women; . . . 'and tell the children of Israel'—this refers to the men" (*Exodus Rabbah* 28:2).

[12] The *Shulchan Aruch* prescribes a feast for circumcision, following the passage in the Talmud, *Shabbat* 130a: "Every precept which [Israel]

accepted with joy, e.g., circumcision . . . they still observe with joy." While it is preferable to perform a *berit milah* in the company of friends and family, a *minyan* is not required.

[13] The term *mohel* (ritual circumciser) is derived from *milah* (circumcision). Commenting on who is allowed to perform a circumcision, Maimonides ruled: "All are permitted to circumcise," including a woman or a non-Jew when there is no *mohel* available (*Yad, Laws of Circumcision* 2:1).

[14] These customs and the definition of these roles varied from one Jewish community to another through the centuries. The role of *sandek* was unknown before the medieval period but became second in importance to the *mohel* in traditional communities. Usually the *sandek* holds the infant on his knees while the *mohel* performs the circumcision.

The *kwater* (derived from the medieval German *Gevatter*, meaning "godfather") and the *kwaterin* (feminine form) traditionally carried the infant from the nursery to the *sandek*. This honor was often given to a childless couple, who thereby assumed a share of the responsibility for raising the child.

Another and an earlier custom is the Chair of Elijah (*Kisei shel Eliyahu*), a chair usually kept in the synagogue and taken to homes for circumcisions in order to symbolize the presence of Elijah. The source of this custom is probably the reference to Elijah in Malachi 3:1 as "the messenger of the covenant." Since Elijah was the messenger of the *berit*, it was only proper that he be present for the occasion.

There are also many local customs as to "traditional" foods to be served at the circumcision meal. All of these are in the realm of custom, and may be observed or not as the family desires.

[15] Jewish tradition ascribes special merit to those who preserve their heritage through the bestowing and retention of Hebrew names. The Midrash states that one of the reasons why the children of Israel deserved to be redeemed from Egyptian bondage was that "they did not change [i.e., Egyptianize] their names; as Reuben and Simeon they descended [Genesis 46] and as Reuben and Simeon they departed [Exodus 1]" (*Leviticus Rabbah* 32:5). The custom of bestowing both a Hebrew and a non-Hebrew name upon a person

goes back to the Bible, e.g., Esther/Hadassah (Esther 2:7) and Daniel/Belteshazzar (Daniel 1:7).

For a more complete discussion of the naming of Jewish children from ancient to modern times, see H. Schauss, *The Lifetime of a Jew,* pp. 12–13, 27–29, 43–48, and 51–53. Lists of Jewish names may be found in the articles on "Naming" in the *Jewish Encyclopedia* (New York, 1905) and the *Encyclopaedia Judaica* (Jerusalem, 1973); in *The Name Dictionary* by Alfred Kolatch (New York, 1967); and in *Ha-Milon He-Hadash* by Even-Shoshan (Jerusalem, 1969), vol. 6.

[16] Among Jews of Middle European and East European origin (i.e., *Ashkenazim*), it is considered proper to name children after deceased relatives. However, among Jews of the Mediterranean lands (i.e., *Sefardim*), there is a rather rigid pattern of naming after living grandparents. And so parents should not be deterred from naming a child after a loved one, living or deceased, because it is "against Jewish custom." We are heir to many different customs in the area of naming.

[17] Children are often given faddish or childish names that are inappropriate and sometimes embarrassing in adulthood. And while Jewish tradition has always ascribed special merit to those who strengthened the Jewish heritage by bestowing and carrying Jewish names (see note 15), it must be mentioned that as far back as the Bible, some Jewish parents gave children "non-Jewish" names, i.e., names typical of the country in which they lived. Moses is an Egyptian name; many of the rabbis of the Mishnah had Greek and Roman names; Saadiah and Maimonides bore names typical of their Arab environment. The Talmud admits ruefully that "the majority of Jews in the Diaspora have names similar to their heathen neighbors" (Talmud B., *Gittin* 11b).

Though we cannot accept the biblical idea that "like his name, so he is" (I Samuel 25:25) as a general rule, surely the name which a person carries through life is of importance and should be chosen thoughtfully. "Every person has three names: the one given by his father and mother, the one that others call him, and the one he acquires for himself" (Midrash, *Ecclesiastes Rabbah* 7:1).

[18] It is a custom of long standing to prepare a *se-udat mitzvah* (a *mitzvah* feast) to celebrate joyous occasions such as the birth of a child, a

circumcision, etc. The traditional literature refers to many such opportunities to share one's joy with the community, e.g., *se-udat Bar Mitzvah* (a feast in honor of a *Bar mitzvah*), *se-udat chatanim* (a feast in honor of bride and groom), *se-udat mazal tov* (lit. a good luck feast, given in honor of the birth of a daughter after her naming). The earliest such feast in honor of a child in Jewish tradition may be found in Genesis 21:8: "Abraham made a great feast on the day that Isaac was weaned."

[19] *Pidyon ha-ben* is based on Exodus 13:1 and 11–15, where Israel is commanded to redeem all male issue who "breach the womb," i.e., who are firstborn to the mother. These firstborn sons are "redeemed" from the priesthood through a ritual in which a *kohen* (descendant of Aaron the priest) is given five shekels. Firstborn sons of priests or Levites are exempt from this ritual, which derives from the ancient custom of dedicating firstborn sons to the priesthood. Since Reform does not recognize a hereditary priesthood and does not believe that firstborn sons should be differentiated in any way from daughters or other sons, this ceremony is incongruous for Reform Jews.

[20] According to most current statutes on adoption in the United States and Canada, adoptive parents have the right to circumcise their child as soon as the initial order of temporary custody has been issued by the court. It is not necessary to wait for the order of permanent custody, which is generally issued six months later. In all such cases one should consult with legal authorities before proceeding.

[21] There are scores of deeply meaningful and beautiful home ceremonies that are a part of the life of the observant Reform Jew. Most of these revolve around the holy days of Judaism. It is strongly recommended that parents keep copies of *Gates of the House, A Shabbat Manual,* and other books on the festivals (for a list of suggestions, see "Basic Library," p. 133) in their homes for ready reference.

[22] "Teaching Torah to the child of another is the same as giving the child life" (Talmud B., *Sanhedrin* 19b).

[23] Hebrew is referred to in Jewish tradition as *leshon ha-kodesh*—the holy language. The Talmud goes so far as to promise the blessings of "the world to come" to those who speak Hebrew (Talmud J., *Shabbat* 1:3).

²⁴ The Torah blessings may be found in the Reform prayerbook, *Gates of Prayer*, page 419, and elsewhere in Hebrew and English. The transliteration may be found on pages 772–73.

²⁵ The meaning of *Bar Mitzvah* is "one who is responsible for the performance of *mitzvot*." The Mishnah refers to a thirteen-year-old as responsible for the fulfillment of *mitzvot* (*Avot* 5:21); elsewhere the Mishnah specifies that a thirteen-year-old is responsible for his own oaths (*Niddah* 5:6). Rabbi Asher ben Yechiel (the most authoritative Jewish legal authority of the thirteenth and fourteenth centuries) in his Responsa established the thirteenth birthday as a basic part of Judaism by asserting: "It is a law given to Moses at Sinai that a male must take responsibility for his transgressions [*bar onshin*] at the age of thirteen and a girl at twelve." In Reform congregations the *Bar/Bat Mitzvah* ceremony is generally conducted for both boys and girls as soon as possible after the thirteenth birthday. Those who observe the tradition of *tefillin* (phylacteries; see Deuteronomy 6:8) begin at age thirteen also.

²⁶ It would be impossible to overstate the importance that our tradition ascribes to lifelong devotion to Jewish studies. "*Talmud Torah* is a greater *mitzvah* than the saving of life . . . than the building of the Temple . . . or than honoring one's father or mother" (Talmud B., *Megillah* 16b). *Pirke Avot* (chap. 6 especially) is full of aphorisms about the value of studying Torah, and Maimonides wrote: "Every Jew, rich or poor or even a beggar, healthy or not, young or old, is obliged to study Torah" (*Yad, Talmud Torah* 1:8).

²⁷ Although there is no unanimous attitude in the Talmud and Midrash toward the *ger* (see note 28), the guiding principle is that he/she should be welcomed and befriended. The following Midrash is typical: "Dearer to God is the proselyte who has come of his own accord than all the crowds of Israelites who stood at Mount Sinai . . ." (*Tanchuma, Lech Lecha* 6).

²⁸ The word *convert* does not describe accurately the process by which one becomes a Jew. *Conversion* is a *religious* term; it says nothing about peoplehood, which is an essential part of Judaism. The proper term for a person who accepts Judaism after a prescribed course of study under the direction of a rabbi or rabbinical court is *ger*

(masculine) or *giyoret* (feminine). These terms are usually translated as "proselyte" or "convert."

[29] In keeping with the idea in note 28 that becoming a *ger* means more than a conversion of faith, notice that Ruth's declaration contains both the element of peoplehood ("your people shall be my people") and the element of faith ("and your God my God").

[30] When Maimonides was asked by a *ger* whether he could recite prayers that include the words "Our God and God of our fathers," he answered: "Yes, . . . in the same way as every Jew by birth says his blessing and prayer, you, too, shall bless and pray. . . . Whoever adopts Judaism and confesses the unity of the Divine Name, as it is prescribed in the Torah, is counted among the disciples of Abraham our Father. . . . For the Torah has been given to us and the proselytes, as it is said, 'One ordinance shall be both for you of the congregation and also for the stranger [*ger*] that sojourns with you. . . . as you are, so shall the stranger be before the Lord' [Numbers 15:15]. . . . Do not consider your origin as inferior. . . . You derive from Him through whose word the world was created" ("Letter to Obadiah the Proselyte," quoted in I. Twersky, *A Maimonides Reader* [New York, 1972]).

[31] The possibility of prejudice against converts was recognized by the early rabbis, and they warned against it quite strongly. "If one is a child of converts, one must not say to him, 'Remember the acts of your ancestors'" (Talmud B., *Baba Metzia* 58b).

The rabbis remind us that Abraham himself was a convert and that his father was an idolater. "One who hurts the feelings of a *ger* transgresses three biblical injunctions . . . 'You shall not wrong a *ger*' [Exodus 22:20]; 'If a *ger* sojourn with you in your land, you shall not wrong him' [Leviticus 19:33]; and 'You shall not therefore wrong each his fellowman' [Leviticus 25:17], a *ger* being included in 'fellowman'" (Talmud B., *Baba Metzia* 59b).

[32] The Midrash teaches: "The father of all converts was Abraham. Therefore, when a convert is named, he/she is named X, son/daughter of our father Abraham" (*Tanchuma, Lech Lecha* 32).

MARRIAGE AND THE JEWISH HOME

[33] Midrash, *Genesis Rabbah* 68:4.

[34] Midrash, *Tehillim* 59.

[35] Talmud B., *Sota* 17a. This passage continues: "but when they are not worthy, fire consumes them." The contrasting of the presence of God in a good marriage with the presence of fire in a bad marriage is derived by the rabbis from the Hebrew words *ish* (man) and *ishah* (woman). Common to both words are ש-א, which spells אש (*esh*)—fire. But when a י is added to אש, changing it to איש (*ish*)—man, and when a ה is added to אש, changing it to אשה (*ishah*)—woman, then we have the completed man and woman. It is not coincidental, the rabbis implied, that these essential letters י and ה together spell יה (*Yah*), i.e., the name of God. And so, they taught, when God is present in the marriage, then it is truly *Kiddushin*—holiness (*Pirke de-Rabbi Eliezer* 12).

[36] See the prayer *Lecha Dodi,* composed in the sixteenth century by Solomon Ha-Levi Alkabetz, in *Gates of Prayer,* pp. 123–25 and 161 (see especially the note at the top of p. 161).

[37] While there is no specific law in the Bible directing people to marry, it is clearly implied in Genesis 2:24 and in all the corollary laws regulating aspects of marriage. Maimonides, in *Sefer Ha-Mitzvot,* lists marriage as one of the 248 positive commandments, deriving it from Deuteronomy 24:1—"When a man takes a wife and marries her . . . "

[38] The talmudic tractate which contains the laws of marriage is called *Kiddushin,* from *kadosh*—sacred or holy. The root meaning of *kadosh* in Hebrew is "set apart," i.e., forbidden to anyone else. Thus the implication of *Kiddushin* is a special relationship, like no other in one's life.

[39] The marriage of a man and a woman in Judaism should be a reflection of the allegorical marriage between God and Israel as described by the prophet Hosea (2:21–22): "I will betroth you unto Me forever; I will betroth you unto Me in righteousness and justice, in loving

kindness and compassion. And I will betroth you unto Me in faithfulness, and you shall know the Lord."

[40] When officiating at a marriage ceremony, the rabbi acts with both religious and civil authority. Since civil law requires the registration of all marriages and authorizes the rabbi to act as an officer of the state for that purpose, the rabbi may not officiate at a marriage without a civil license nor may he fail to register the marriage with the proper state agency. The principle of *Dina de-malchuta dina* ("The law of the government is the law," i.e., it is binding on Jews; see Talmud B., *Gittin* 10b) applies here; since the civil law requires the licensing and registration of marriages, the rabbi is forbidden to officiate unless the couple complies with these civil requirements.

[41] Recent medical research has identified certain diseases, some of them fatal, to which Jews in particular may be highly susceptible. A 1975 resolution of the CCAR calls upon all rabbis "to urge those couples seeking their officiating at marriage ceremonies to undergo screening for Tay-Sachs and other genetic diseases which afflict Jews to a significant degree."

[42] Rabbinic tradition has it that King Solomon built special gates into the Temple for bridegrooms and mourners so that the people could greet them and share their joy or sorrow. Bridegrooms would be greeted with these words: " 'May He who dwells in this house cause you to rejoice with sons and daughters.' . . . When the Temple was destroyed, the sages instituted the rule that bridegrooms and mourners should go to the synagogues and to the houses of study. The people would see the bridegroom there and rejoice with him . . ." (*Pirke de-Rabbi Eliezer* 17; also see Talmud B., *Soferim* 19:12). This is the origin of going to the synagogue for a blessing on the Sabbath before a wedding. In the spirit of Reform Judaism, the blessing is, of course, extended to both bridegroom and bride.

[43] It would be wrong to state unequivocally that all Jewish authorities prescribed joyful, enthusiastic, and regular sexual intercourse in marriage. But considering the puritanical voices through history that have suggested the opposite attitude toward sex in marriage, it is noteworthy how many Jewish authorities have understood sexuality to be a gift of God to be accepted with gratitude and joy. This

attitude of joy in marital sex may be found in many talmudic passages, notably *Nedarim* 20b, *Niddah* 31a–b, *Yevamot* 34b, *Sanhedrin* 85b, etc. The fact that the Talmud in several instances allows a woman to use a contraceptive (*moch;* see *Yevamot* 12b and 100a, *Ketubot* 39a, *Niddah* 45a, etc.) indicates that intercourse was allowed for the sake of conjugal pleasure. For a fuller discussion, see "The Mitzvah of Marital Sex" and "The Legitimacy of Sexual Pleasure" in David Feldman, *Birth Control in Jewish Law* (New York, 1968), pp. 60–105.

Three rabbinic texts touching on aspects of conjugal relations are worthy of note (see also "A Jewish View of Sexuality, p. 127):

    a. *Talmud Jerushalmi, Kiddushin* 4:12: "A person will be held accountable to God for refusing to enjoy those pleasures that are permitted to him."

    b. *Iggeret Ha-Kodesh* (attributed to Nachmanides, 13th cent.). "Intercourse is a holy and pure thing when done in an appropriate way, in an appropriate time, and with appropriate intention. . . . We believe that God created all things in accordance with His wisdom. . . . if our sexual organs are a disgrace, how could it happen that God created something shameful or ugly?"

    c. *Pesikta Rabbati* 17b: "The Torah teaches gentle manners; the bridegroom should not enter the marriage chamber until the bride gives him permission."

[44] "No amount of modern Jewish apologetic, endlessly poured forth, can alter the fact that the Rabbinic attitude towards women was very different from our own. No amount of apologetics can get over the implications of the daily blessing, which Orthodox Judaism . . . [still retains]: Blessed art thou, O Lord our God, who has not made me a woman.' At the same time it must be readily admitted that the Rabbis seem to have loved their wives, that they all, apparently, had only one wife each, and that the position of the wife was one of much influence and importance" (Montefiore and Loewe, *A Rabbinic Anthology,* p. 507).

In studying even those passages in rabbinic texts that are most complimentary and protective of women, one notes immediately that the focus is the man, e.g., "A man who has no wife lives without joy, blessing, and good" (*Yevamot* 62b) or "Be careful about the honor of your wife, for blessing enters the home only because of the wife" (*Baba Metzia* 59a). These are very noble sentiments, but they are unquestionably male-centered.

In the traditional wedding service, it is still the man who takes the woman to be his wife; she is consecrated to him; there is no mutuality. In traditional Judaism the prerogative in divorce belongs to the man almost exclusively; a bereaved woman, not a man, is subject to the indignities of *yibbum* and *chalitzah* (levirate marriage and the ceremony required to avoid it; see Deuteronomy 25:5–10); a woman whose husband disappears or whose death has not been witnessed becomes an *agunah* (lit. restrained, i.e., forbidden ever to remarry); and control of the family in general is vested in the husband. The emphasis on the absolute equality of man and woman is one of the significant contributions of Reform Judaism.

[45] Talmud B., *Yevamot* 21a, derived from Leviticus 18:6–18. Since civil law and Jewish tradition are not identical in this area, it would be wise to consult one's rabbi.

[46] The phrase "major festival" refers to all those holy days called *mikra-ei kodesh*—holy convocations—in Leviticus 23:2 *et seq.*: Shabbat (23:3); the first day of Pesach (23:7); the last day of Pesach (23:8); Shavuot (23:21); Rosh Ha-Shanah (23:24); Yom Kippur (23:27); the first day of Sukkot (23:35); Shemini Atzeret (Simchat Torah) (23:36).

[47] Tish'a Be-Av (lit. the ninth day of the Hebrew month Av) is the traditional day of fasting and mourning in commemoration of the destruction of the two Temples in ancient Jerusalem as well as subsequent tragedies in Jewish history.

Yom Ha-Shoah is Holocaust Day, the twenty-seventh of Nissan, commemorating the destruction of European Jewry by the Nazis before and during World War II.

[48] Some rabbis will also refrain from officiating at marriages on several other days when tradition prescribes that no wedding take place: the intermediate days of Pesach and Sukkot, the days of the Counting of the *Omer*, and the three-week period preceding Tish'a Be-Av.

The Counting of the *Omer* begins on the second evening of Pesach and continues for forty-nine days through the day before

Shavuot. Orthodox and traditional rabbis will not officiate at weddings during most of this period, which since the days of the Roman persecution has been considered a time of mourning. (There are several exceptional days during this period when weddings may be held, even by traditional rabbis: Lag Be-Omer, Rosh Chodesh, and the last three days of the counting.)

The three-week period before Tish'a Be-Av is traditionally referred to as *Bein Ha-Metzarim* (*in extremis;* see Lamentations 1:3), i.e, the period between the day when the walls of Jerusalem were breached by the Babylonians (the seventeenth of Tammuz) and Tish'a Be-Av. The Orthodox observe certain mourning customs during this entire period including the abstention from weddings.

[49] This prohibition derives from the need to be absolutely certain about the paternity of a potential child.

[50] Jewish tradition refers to both the home and the synagogue as *mikdash me-at*—miniature sanctuary (see section E).

[51] The *Shulchan Aruch* prescribes that the marriage ceremony take place in the open air whenever possible (*Even Ha-Ezer* 61:1).

[52] At most Reform wedding ceremonies the rabbi will recite the *Sheva Berachot* (the traditional seven blessings, which are first noted in Talmud B., *Ketubot* 7b–8a) or a variant of them. These *berachot* are as follows: (a) for wine, (b) for creation, (c) for the creation of humankind, (d) for the creation of the human capacity for reproduction, (e) for the future joy of Zion and her children, (f) for the joy of groom and bride, and (g) for love, kinship, peace, friendship, and the joyous sounds of grooms and brides at feast in redeemed Jerusalem. (See the essay on *Kiddushin,* p. 123.)

In talmudic times the marriage ceremony was divided into two distinct parts, often held a year apart (probably deriving from biblical custom; see Deuteronomy 20:7). The first part was called *Eirusin,* or betrothal, and the second part was called *Nisuin,* or marriage. During the Middle Ages these two ceremonies were combined as they are in the Orthodox ceremony today, the only vestiges of their former separateness being the recitation of two introductory *berachot*—the first for wine and the second for the laws concerning whom one may or may not betroth—over the first of two goblets of wine.

[53] Several features of the marriage arrangement between Rebekah and Isaac in Genesis 24 provided the basis for later Jewish marriage customs, e.g., the necessity of the bride's consent (vv. 57–58), the veil (v. 65), etc. (see the brief essay "On Marriage" following the story of Rebekah's betrothal, in W. Gunther Plaut, *The Torah: A Modern Commentary,* vol. 1, p. 240). In Central and Eastern Europe it was (and among some still is) customary for the groom and the officiant to go to the place where the bride and her attendants were waiting and to cover her face with a veil. This was called *bedecken* in certain communities, and it was accompanied by the groom or others saying to the bride: "O sister, may you grow into thousands of myriads . . ." (Genesis 24:60).

[54] The use of a *chuppah,* or marriage canopy, may or may not be observed by Reform Jews. Usually it consists of a piece of material, possibly a *tallit,* suspended on four poles above the heads of the couple during the ceremony. (In some communities a *tallit* is draped over the shoulders of bride and groom.) The *chuppah* symbolizes the marriage chamber in which the couple share conjugal privacy. According to the Talmud, the bride is considered married from the moment that she steps under the *chuppah* (*Ketubot* 48a–b; see especially *Tosafot* commentary, bottom 48a; see also *Yad, Laws of Marriage* 4:2).

[55] In the Bible and the Talmud there is mention of the presence of the best friends of the bride and the groom at the wedding ceremony, but the custom of *unterführer,* couples to escort the groom and the bride to the *chuppah,* is relatively modern. See the description in H. Schauss, *The Lifetime of a Jew,* pp. 187–88.

[56] The breaking of the glass probably derives from ancient psycho-sexual symbolism. It is a feature of most traditional weddings, and many Reform Jews prefer to retain it while giving it a variety of interpretations, e.g., that it represents the destruction of the Temple and the tragedies of Jewish history and thus links the new couple to the Jewish people, whether in sadness or in joy (this is the interpretation found in most traditional sources, derived from Psalms 137:6); that

it represents our fragmented society, where so many are in need, and suggests that the couple can find happiness only if they work toward the betterment of the world; that it represents the fragility of the marriage bond and, therefore, the need for love and understanding if the marriage is to survive and flourish; etc. (For a detailed study of this subject, see J. Z. Lauterbach's essay, "The Ceremony of Breaking a Glass at Weddings," *HUC Annual,* 1925, pp. 351–380.)

[57] The traditional declaration by the groom is derived from Talmud B., *Kiddushin* 5b–6a.

[58] According to tradition, the wedding ring must be smooth and of clearly determinable value since it is with the ring that the groom "acquires" the bride, i.e., for value received. Since Reform Judaism does not consider the presentation of the ring to be an act through which the groom acquires the bride, it makes no difference what the ring is made of, whether or not it is engraved, or whether or not it has stones.

[59] The witnesses at a Jewish wedding should be adults, Jewish, and not related by blood to either the bride or the groom (*Shulchan Aruch, Even Ha-Ezer* 42:5). While the tradition requires male witnesses, in a Reform ceremony both men and women may serve in this capacity.

[60] Aramaic was the *lingua franca* of the North Semitic peoples for most of the period from the fourth pre-Christian century to the sixth or seventh century of our era. It is a language closely related to Hebrew and was used as the vernacular and in legal documents by most Jews during that period. Much of the Babylonian Talmud is written in Aramaic.

[61] See the essay on *tzedakah* in the Appendix, p. 121.

[62] The earliest laws of divorce in Judaism may be found in the Torah (Deuteronomy 24:1–4) and in the talmudic tractate on divorce, *Gittin.* See the essay on divorce in the Appendix, p. 136.

[63] The talmudic tractate on divorce, after ninety folios covering all its legal ramifications, concludes with the words: "If a man divorces his first wife, even the altar sheds tears" (*Gittin* 90b).

[64] In traditional Judaism a person who has only a civil but not a religious

divorce (*get*) is not considered divorced. Subsequent remarriage by such a person and the legitimacy of the children of such a remarriage will be questioned wherever traditional law is binding (as, for example, in Israel).

The traditional process for acquiring a *get* is complex and requires the convening of a rabbinical court (*bet din*) and the services of a scribe (Sofer). A *get* is usually issued by a rabbinical court only after a civil divorce has been granted.

[65] There are many biblical passages forbidding marriage between Jews and non-Jews (generally idolaters), e.g., "You shall not intermarry with them" (in this case "them" refers to the Canaanite nations); "you shall not give your daughter to his son, and you shall not take his daughter for your son" (Deuteronomy 7:3; see also Exodus 34:16, Joshua 23:12, Ezra 9:1–2 and 10:10–11, and Nehemiah 10:31).

Maimonides includes the prohibition against intermarriage among the 365 negative commandments in *Sefer Ha-Mitzvot,* basing himself on Deuteronomy 7:3 and on the statement in the Talmud: "The prohibition against marrying their daughters is a biblical ordinance" (*Avodah Zarah* 36b; see also *Sanhedrin* 81b).

From time to time rabbinic authorities discussed whether or not the prohibition against intermarriage with heathens should apply to intermarriage with Christians or Moslems, but the question was usually a moot one in that the predominant Christian and Moslem authorities forbade intermarriage with Jews.

The American Reform rabbinate made its first statement on this subject at its 1909 convention: ". . . mixed marriages are contrary to the tradition of the Jewish religion and should therefore be discouraged." This position was reiterated by the CCAR in 1947 and 1973. For a detailed view of interfaith marriage, see S. Seltzer, *Jews and Non-Jews Falling in Love* (UAHC, 1976).

[66] The terms *mixed marriage* and *intermarriage* are often used interchangeably. *Intermarriage* is defined by sociologists as a marriage in which the two parties were born into different religious or ethnic communities, whether or not there has been a conversion. According to Jewish tradition, however, a marriage between a Jew and a former non-Jew who has converted to Judaism is a Jewish marriage. The methods of conversion used in the Orthodox, Conservative, and

Reform communities may differ, but once a proper conversion has taken place, the formerly non-Jewish partner is Jewish in every way, and therefore the marriage is not an intermarriage.

A *mixed marriage* is one in which the two parties were born into different religious communities and in which no conversion has taken place. The Reform rabbinate has spoken out against mixed marriage (see note 65) and has declared its "opposition to participation by its members in any ceremony which solemnizes a mixed marriage" (CCAR Resolution, 1973).

This sensitive matter has generated considerable discussion among Reform rabbis and no unanimity prevails, but most Reform rabbis are of the opinion that they cannot invoke the traditional formula for marriage, *kedat Mosheh ve-Yisrael* ("according to the tradition of Moses and Israel"; see C-3 above), for persons to whom that tradition does not apply. It should be noted that the opposition of Judaism to mixed marriage has nothing to do with the legitimacy of the marriage or the "salvation" of the non-Jewish partner. Every marriage solemnized by competent religious or civil authority is legally valid, and most Reform congregations will accept as members families in which one member is not Jewish. The CCAR Resolution of 1973 on Mixed Marriage calls on Reform rabbis to help educate the children of mixed marriages as Jews and to help bring these families into the Jewish community.

[67] "How goodly are your tents, O Jacob; your dwelling places, O Israel" (Numbers 24:5). This poetic parallelism suggests that the houses of study (synagogues) and the homes of the Jewish people are its twin sources of strength.

[68] While the synagogue replaced the ancient Temple as the primary locus of Jewish worship, the Jewish home is considered a "miniature sanctuary," and Judaism teaches that God is as much in the home, the marketplace, and the school as in the synagogue. Rabbi Mendel of Kotzk taught: "Where is God? Wherever you let him in" (quoted in *Gates of Prayer*, p. 8).

[69] "Speak of them in your home and on your way, when you lie down and when you rise up" (Deuteronomy 6:6).

[70] Maimonides includes the *mezuzah* among the 248 positive command-

ments in his *Sefer Ha-Mitzvot,* deriving it from "You shall write them on the doorposts of your house and your gates" (Deuteronomy 6:9). The word *mezuzah* means "doorpost." "The purpose of the *mezuzah* is to consecrate the Jewish home as a temple of God" (S. R. Hirsch, *Nineteen Letters,* no. 13, 1836).

[71] Rabbi Jacob ben Moses Mölln (14th cent., Mainz; known as the Maharil), at the conclusion of his collection of laws related to the *mezuzah,* gives the following reason for the slanting position of the *mezuzah:* Rashi (the great eleventh-century commentator) and his grandson, Rabbenu Tam, came to opposite conclusions as to the proper placement of the *mezuzah.* Rashi stated that it should be attached to the doorpost in a horizontal position, and Rabbenu Tam stated that it should be vertical. Maharil ruled that we should not contravene either of these great authorities and therefore that we should compromise, affixing the *mezuzah* on the diagonal. In keeping with the spirit of this tradition, the *mezuzah* may also serve as a symbol of compromise, i.e., that those who live in a house where a *mezuzah* is affixed to the doorpost are willing to compromise for the sake of *shelom bayit*—family harmony.

[72] Maimonides, *Yad, Mezuzah* 5:4, where it says that those who consider the *mezuzah* a charm to ward off evil are in error. The real purpose of the *mezuzah* is to make a person aware, every time that he enters or leaves his home, of the unity of God and his moral obligations as a believer in God.

[73] "Torah" in its broader sense includes not only the Five Books of Moses but all those books that might be identified as sacred scripture, e.g., the rest of the Bible, the Talmud and Midrash, and the writings of Jewish scholars through the ages that were inspired by the Torah.

[74] "You shall eat and be satisfied and bless the Lord your God . . ." (Deuteronomy 8:10). This passage, which indicates that mealtime should be much more than an occasion to fill one's stomach, is contrasted with the Genesis passage which cites, as an example of Esau's wicked contempt for his birthright, the crude manner in which he ate: "And Jacob gave Esau bread and lentil soup; and he ate and drank and got up and left; thus did Esau despise his birthright" (Genesis 25:34). The implication is that if he were the true spiritual

heir of Abraham and Isaac, he would have taken the time to thank God for his food rather than leave abruptly as soon as his stomach was full.

[75] In rabbinical writings the family table is often compared to the altar of the Temple. It is for this reason that the custom arose to sprinkle salt on the bread or *challah* after *Ha-Motsi,* as we read in Leviticus (2:13): "You shall offer salt along with all your sacrificial offerings." Also in keeping with the analogy of the table to the altar is the tradition of utilizing mealtimes for study; "If three have eaten at a table and have spoken no words of Torah, it is as if they had partaken of sacrifices to dead idols . . ." (Mishnah, *Avot* 3:4).

[76] Maimonides includes the recitation of the Sabbath *Kiddush* at the family table as one of the 248 positive commandments in *Sefer Ha-Mitzvot.* He derives it from "Remember the Sabbath day to keep it holy" (Exodus 20:8). "To keep it holy" in Hebrew is *le-kadesho.* "This is the commandment of *Kiddush,*" according to Maimonides.

[77] The custom of blessing children goes back to the very origins of Judaism; see the blessing of Jacob and Esau by Isaac (Genesis 27) and the blessing of the twelve sons and two grandsons by Jacob (Genesis 48–49).

[78] The traditional blessing for sons is taken from Genesis 48:20, and the concluding three-verse blessing is the traditional *Birkat Kohanim* (Priestly Benediction), Numbers 6:24–26.

[79] The Talmud (*Shabbat* 127a), elaborating on the Mishnah (*Peah* 1:1), lists *hachnasat orchim* among those *mitzvot* for which "a person is rewarded in this world and in the world to come." One does not have to believe in physical reward and punishment to accept the idea that the performance of *hachnasat orchim* (and the other humanitarian *mitzvot* on this list; see also *Gates of Prayer,* p. 285) is eternally rewarding.

In the same talmudic passage, Rabbi Judah went even further in praise of *hachnasat orchim,* teaching that "welcoming guests is of greater merit even than welcoming the presence of God." Today, considering the great number of fragmented families and single adults in our society (see "The Single Person, the Single-Parent Family, and *Mitzvot,*" p. 119) and the particular difficulty that such people have in observing home-centered *mitzvot*, it is of the greatest importance to include them in *chavurot* (congregational subgroups which meet to study Judaism and/or celebrate Shabbat and festivals) and to invite them into the family circle.

[80] There are many statements in rabbinic literature about the centrality of the synagogue. Among these are: "Whosoever has a fixed place for his prayer has the God of Abraham as his helper"; "A person's prayer is heard only in the synagogue"; and "When a person leaves the synagogue, he should not walk hastily . . . but when he goes to the synagogue, it is a *mitzvah* to rush" (Talmud B., *Berachot* 6a–b).

The synagogue as we know it is, of course, a post-biblical institution, and as such there could be no biblical *mitzvah* to join or attend a synagogue, but the rabbis used several biblical verses as *ex post facto* underpinnings for the centrality of the synagogue; for example: "What is the meaning of the verse 'But as for me, let my prayer come to You, O Lord, in an acceptable time' [Psalms 69:14]? When is 'an acceptable time'? When the congregation is praying" (*Berachot* 8a). And, of course, there is the famous dictum of Hillel: "Do not separate yourself from the congregation" (Mishnah, *Avot* 2:5).

DEATH AND MOURNING

[81] Joshua Loth Liebman, as quoted in *Gates of Prayer,* p. 625.

[82] *Shulchan Aruch, Yoreh Deah* 394. The Talmud imposes clear limits on the various periods of grief (see note 121) and suggests that God says to those who choose to mourn excessively: "You should not be more compassionate to the dead than I am" (Talmud B., *Moed Katan* 27b).

[83] Jewish tradition prescribes a multitude of acts, from the bedside vigil to shoveling earth into the grave, which underscore the reality of death. Modern psychological insight confirms the wisdom of such funeral and mourning procedures, emphasizing that "the recognition of death is a necessity for continuing life, and grief is a necessary and unavoidable process in normative psychological functioning" (Vivian M. Rakoff, "Psychiatric Aspects of Death in America," in *Death in American Experience* [New York, 1974]).

[84] "Where there is no one to attend to the burial of a corpse, it is called a *met mitzvah* [a dead person whose burial is a commandment], that is to say, a corpse whose burial is obligatory upon every person . . ." (Maimonides, *Sefer Ha-Mitzvot,* Positive #231). Maimonides derives this *mitzvah* from Deuteronomy 21:23—"You shall surely bury him . . ."

[85] Commenting on the mishnaic rule that food should not be brought to a house of mourning on trays or salvers or in fancy baskets, but rather in plain baskets, the Talmud says: "Formerly they would bring food to the house of mourning, the rich in silver and gold baskets and the poor in baskets of willow twigs, and the poor felt shamed. They therefore instituted that all should bring food in baskets of willow twigs, out of deference to the poor. . . .

"Formerly they would bring out the rich for burial on stately beds and the poor on plain biers, and the poor felt shamed. They therefore instituted that all should be brought out on plain biers, out of deference to the poor. . . .

"Formerly the expense of burying the dead was a greater blow to the family than the death itself, so that the dead person's kin would abandon him. Finally, Rabban Gamliel came forward and, disregarding his own dignity, gave orders that he [himself] be buried in plain linen garments. Thereafter the people followed his example and all were buried in linen garments . . ." (Talmud B., *Moed Katan* 27a–b).

[86] Testament of Job 38:11. Also in the Apocrypha we read: "Cultivate the physician as you need him, for him too has God ordained" (Ben Sira 38:1).

[87] The Talmud (*Shabbat* 127a), elaborating on the Mishnah (*Peah* 1:1), lists *bikkur cholim* as one of the ten basic *mitzvot* for which "a person is rewarded in this world and in the world to come." See also note 79.

[88] "A person who visits the sick helps them to recover" (Talmud B., *Nedarim* 40a).

[89] The Talmud teaches: "If one falls sick and his life is in danger, he is told, 'Make confession,' for all who are sentenced to death make confession" (*Shabbat* 32a). The traditional prayer of confession, *Viddui*, implies that the death of a person will serve as an atonement for his sins (Talmud B., *Sanhedrin* 43b).

The prayer for the critically ill in the Reform *Gates of the House* (p. 128) is based on the traditional *Viddui*, but it does not suggest that death serves as an atonement for sin. Rather it asks for the "courage to accept whatever befalls me" and for God's protection over loved ones, and concludes with an affirmation of faith.

[90] Judaism forbids the taking of life except in self-defense and in the case where one person is pursuing another to kill him. The "pursuer" is considered a murderer and may be killed. (This principle is also applied to a fetus whose birth might result in the death of the mother. Such a fetus is considered a "pursuer" and may be killed; see "Birth," A-3.)

The act of killing a sick person for whatever reason is absolutely forbidden. According to the *Shulchan Aruch,* even when a person is dying, he may not be disturbed in any way that might hasten his death (*Yoreh Deah* 339).

[91] While Jewish tradition forbids any overt act to hasten death, most authorities agree that nothing need be done to keep a dying person alive artificially. The classic story is that of Rabbi Judah the Prince, who was being kept alive by the unceasing prayers of his colleagues (Talmud B., *Ketubot* 104a). A servant, recognizing that the case was hopeless and that Rabbi Judah was in great pain, diverted the

rabbis' attention so that they stopped praying, and Rabbi Judah died peacefully.

In the *Sefer Chasidim* (13th cent.) it says: "If a person is sick and in pain and dying and asks another person to kill him mercifully, this request must not be fulfilled, nor may the person take his own life. *Still, you may not put salt on his tongue to keep him alive longer"* (p. 10, #315–18). Putting salt on the tongue was believed to be a method of prolonging life.

[92] There are many examples of ethical wills in rabbinic literature. The Talmud quotes Rabbi Judah the Prince's final moral instructions to his sons. It is a classical example of an ethical will: "When Rabbi was about to die, he said, 'I require the presence of my sons.' When his sons entered, he instructed them: 'Take care that you show due respect to your mother. The light shall continue to burn in its usual place, the table shall be laid in its usual place, and my bed shall be spread in its usual place . . .' " (*Ketubot* 103a).

The custom of leaving or speaking an ethical will for one's children actually goes back to the Bible (see Genesis 49, esp. v. 33; 40:24–25; and Deuteronomy 33). The medieval ethical wills of Maimonides, Nachmanides, and Rabbi Judah He-Chasid are particularly noteworthy, as are the more recent wills of the Vilna Gaon and Rabbi Moses Sofer and the three examples quoted in the Appendix.

[93] This prayer in shortened form—*Baruch Dayan ha-emet*—is prescribed in the Mishnah (*Berachot* 9:2) on the occasion of "hearing bad news." Later authorities, especially the *Shulchan Aruch* (*Yoreh Deah* 339), prescribed the prayer in its fuller form to be recited by the family as soon as death occurred.

[94] The term *Tzidduk Ha-Din* as a justification of the divine decree of death is first used in the Talmud in a passage describing how Rabbi Chananya ben Teradion (2nd cent.), his wife, and his daughter were sentenced to death by the Romans. "As the three of them went out [from the Roman tribunal], they declared their submission to righteous judgment [i.e., God's will]." The passage proceeds to describe how each of the three quoted verses from the Bible (Deuteronomy 32:4 and Jeremiah 32:19), which thereupon became part of the Jewish burial service. "Rabba said: 'How great were these righteous ones in that the three scriptural passages expressing submission to

divine justice [i.e., *Tzidduk Ha-Din*] readily occurred to them just at the appropriate time for the declaration of such submission'" (*Avodah Zarah* 18a).

[95] *Pikuach nefesh*—the saving of a life—is the most urgent *mitzvah* in Judaism. "Nothing must take precedence over saving a life" (Talmud B., *Yoma* 82a). There is a general principle in traditional Judaism (based on the Talmud, *Sanhedrin* 47b) that the body of the dead may not be used for the benefit of the living. But most modern Orthodox authorities agree that the prohibitions on deriving benefit from the dead may be set aside in cases of *pikuach nefesh* and that organ transplants are permitted even in cases where the recipient is not in imminent danger of death (see responsa of Rabbi I. Y. Unterman, *Shevet Mi-Yehudah,* pp. 313 *et seq.,* and Rabbi Solomon B. Freehof, *Contemporary Reform Responsa,* pp. 216–23).

[96] Respect for the dead and reverence for the human body are major principles of Jewish law; consequently autopsies were strictly forbidden by the early rabbis. However, when the principle of *pikuach nefesh* (see note 95) comes into conflict with the reverence due a dead body, *pikuach nefesh* takes precedence. Thus, we find that most Orthodox authorities after the eighteenth century permit autopsies in cases where there is a clear benefit to the health of others to be derived from the autopsy. Particularly interesting in this regard is the agreement reached in 1944 between the Chief Rabbi of Palestine and the Chief Rabbi of Jerusalem and Dr. Chaim Yassky of the Hadassah Hospital "permitting autopsies in the following cases: (1) When the civil law demanded it in cases of crime and accidental death; (2) To establish the cause of death when it was doubtful; (3) In order to save lives; and (4) In cases of hereditary disease" (*Encyclopaedia Judaica,* vol. 3, col. 932).

[97] For a complete discussion of the matter of donating one's body to science from both the traditional and Reform points of view, see the following responsa by Solomon B. Freehof: *Reform Responsa,* pp. 130 f.; *Modern Reform Responsa,* pp. 278 f.; and *Contemporary Reform Responsa,* pp. 216 f.

[98] It is understood that before the coffin is closed a member of the family or their representative will have established the identity of the body.

[99] The Talmud (*Moed Katan* 24a) and the *Shulchan Aruch* (*Yoreh Deah* 340:1) require the rending of one's clothes (actually the symbolic rending of the upper part of one's outer garment) on the death of one's parent, wife, child, or sibling. The custom is an ancient one and is often mentioned in the Bible (e.g., Genesis 37:34, when Jacob heard about the alleged death of Joseph). For the Reform Jew the cutting or tearing of a garment or ribbon might be appropriate as an act of grief, as a reminder of loss, and as a means of informing others of one's recent tragedy.

[100] The Talmud (*Shabbat* 127a), elaborating on the *Mishnah* (*Peah* 1:1), lists *halvayat ha-met* (accompanying the dead; see C-9) as one of the ten *mitzvot* for which "a person is rewarded in this world and in the world to come."

[101] Chapter 23 of Genesis is the first reference to burial in the Bible. In it we read of the great concern of the patriarch Abraham for a proper burial place for his wife, Sarah, and how he, as the principal mourner, took care of this sacred task himself. The fact that Isaac, Sarah's only son, is not mentioned in chapter 23 as being involved in the burial gave rise to several rabbinic legends explaining his absence.

[102] See note 84 above.

[103] Maimonides, basing himself on the commandment to bury the corpse of an executed criminal on the day of death (Deuteronomy 21:23), extends this to all Jews: ". . . every Israelite must be buried on the day of his death" (*Sefer Ha-Mitzvot*, Positive #231). Such haste, though, was recognized in the *Shulchan Aruch* as not always possible or advisable. "One may leave the body overnight if it is for the honor of the dead, e.g., to procure a coffin and shrouds or to await the arrival of relatives. . . . the Torah forbade any delay in burial only when such delay would indicate contempt for the dead, but we may delay for the honor of the dead" (*Shulchan Aruch, Yoreh Deah* 357).

[104] See note 46 above.

[105] Most Orthodox and Conservative Jews (outside of Israel) observe a second day for all the festivals (see note 46) listed in Leviticus 23 except Shabbat and Yom Kippur. Since certain members of the family

and the Jewish community might observe the second day, it would be best to consult with the rabbi. However, even among traditional Jews, burial on the second day of a festival is allowed in some cases.

[106] See note 85 above.

[107] Funeral orations or eulogies go back to antiquity in Judaism (see II Samuel 1:17–27 and 3:33–34). In talmudic times they were commonplace: "From the funeral eulogy pronounced over a man we know whether eternal life is his or not" (*Shabbat* 153a).

[108] Traditionally eulogies were not offered and the funeral service itself was abridged if burial took place on a Friday, the eve of a festival, or a day when there was no mourning (i.e., a semi-holy day like the New Moon, Purim, Chanukah).

[109] See note 100 above.

[110] Burial is one of the most ancient traditions in Judaism. "Dust you are and to the dust you will return" (Genesis 3:19); the Bible refers to burial in several instances, beginning with the burial of Sarah by Abraham (Genesis 23). However, burial as described in the Bible and the Mishnah often seems to refer to interment in caves and rock niches (see Isaiah 22:16 and Mishnah, *Baba Batra* 6:8). Most post-mishnaic authorities indicate earth burial as the proper Jewish mode of interment, and this became the norm as described in *Shulchan Aruch, Yoreh Deah* 362.

[111] For a more complete discussion of the question of the proper disposal of cremation ashes, see Solomon B. Freehof's *Contemporary Reform Responsa,* pp. 169–72.

[112] See K. Kohler, *CCAR Yearbook* vol. 24, p. 154.

[113] According to tradition, a quorum of ten Jewish men—a *minyan*—is required for the recitation of certain prayers, among them *Kaddish.*
    A *minyan* is not required in Reform Judaism, but it is certainly desirable in that it emphasizes the importance of community. Women are, of course, counted equally in a Reform *minyan.*

[114] The *mitzvah* of *Kaddish* is described in D-7 and in a brief essay in the Appendix, page 143.

[115] The primary consideration here is suicide. Tradition forbade the burial of suicides in Jewish cemeteries and the performance of mourning rites for them. The governing talmudic text is: "If one destroys himself consciously, we do not involve ourselves with his funeral . . . and we do not say a eulogy for him . . ." (Talmud B., *Semachot* 2:1). Today even Orthodox Jews find ways to interpret the law more liberally. In Reform Judaism there should be no distinction between suicides and others.

[116] "Mourning rites are not withheld in any respect from one who fell into the sea or was carried away by a stream or killed by a wild beast" (Talmud B., *Semachot* 2:12).

[117] The question of mourning for a person who has disappeared is related to the problem of the *agunah* (a woman whose husband has disappeared and who, according to tradition, is forbidden to remarry because of the chance that he might be alive; see note 44). According to Reform Judaism, if the civil authorities declare that a person is dead, mourning rites are observed and the widow is free to remarry.

[118] There is no specific law in the Torah about mourning for one's dead. Maimonides, however, does include it as a positive commandment, deriving it from the law of the *kohen* who must defile himself for his immediate relatives (Leviticus 21:23). "On this commandment is based the duty of mourning; i.e., the obligation incumbent upon every Israelite man to mourn after the loss of relatives, who are six in number" (i.e., mother, father, son, daughter, brother, and sister; mourning by and for husband and wife is a rabbinic extension; *Sefer Ha-Mitzvot*, Positive #37). The many complex laws in the Talmud regulating aspects of mourning make it clear that the early Rabbis considered mourning for those enumerated above as a *mitzvah*.

[119] Mishnah, *Sanhedrin* 6:6.

[120] "One whose dead relative lies before him [i.e., has not yet been buried] is exempt from the recital of the *Shema* . . . and from all the *mitzvot* in the Torah. . . . On Sabbath, however, he may recline and eat meat and drink wine . . . and he is subject to all the *mitzvot* in the Torah" (Talmud B., *Berachot* 17b–18a).

[121] The Talmud takes a text from the prophet Jeremiah as the basis for

its regulation regarding periods of intense mourning. " 'Do not weep for the dead or bemoan him' [Jeremiah 22:10]. 'Do not weep for the dead' means excessively [i.e., do not weep excessively]; 'or bemoan him' means beyond measure [i.e., do not bemoan him beyond measure]. How is this understood? Three days for weeping and seven for lamenting and thirty to refrain from cutting one's hair and wearing pressed clothes [i.e., thirty days during which one should not have to worry about one's personal appearance]. Thereafter, the Holy One, blessed be He, says: 'You should not be more compassionate toward the departed than I' " (*Moed Katan* 27b).

[122] According to tradition, if burial occurs before a festival, the festival cancels the *shivah,* i.e., the mourner is relieved of the necessity to follow the customs of *shivah* (see D-2). If, on the other hand, burial occurs during the intermediate days of Passover or Sukkot, tradition prescribes the observance of the full *shivah* period after the festival (*Moed Katan* 19a; *Shulchan Aruch, Yoreh Deah* 399).

[123] Tradition pictures God Himself as setting the example in the comforting of mourners (see note 121). The Talmud teaches that "God Himself in all His glory went to console Isaac when his father, Abraham, died" (*Sotah* 14a).

There are several instances of consolation in the Bible. Possibly the most instructive is the story of Job's comforters: "They sat down upon the ground with him seven days and seven nights, but none of them spoke a word to him, for they saw how great was his suffering" (Job 2:11–13). The rabbis took this verse to teach that one should not speak to a mourner until he is ready, as the Talmud says: "Silence is meritorious in a house of mourning" (*Berachot* 6b).

[124] The custom of including a Torah lesson in the service in a house of mourning probably developed from the notion that *mitzvot* done in the name of the deceased would help their souls to rise to Paradise. *Talmud Torah*—learning Torah—is considered the equal of all other *mitzvot* combined (Mishnah, *Peah* 1:1), and the Talmud teaches that "all sins are forgiven the person who studies Torah" (*Berachot* 5a). And so, just as tradition taught that the faithful recitation of the *Kaddish* (Mishnah, *Eduyot* 2:10; also see the essay on *Kaddish* in the Appendix) would help the soul to ascend, the performance of

the *mitzvah* of *Talmud Torah* in the name of the deceased and in his home would surely help.

Reform Judaism does not teach that *mitzvot* help dead souls to rise, but it does teach that Torah study is a *mitzvah*. What more appropriate way could there be to memorialize a loved one than to use the occasion of the *shivah minyan* to study Torah?

[125] See Talmud, *Moed Katan* 27a and note 85 above.

[126] The custom of lighting a candle in memory of the dead is related by some to the biblical verse "The spirit of man is the light of the Lord" (Proverbs 20:27).

[127] See the brief essay on *Kaddish* in the Appendix (p. 143).

[128] While Reform Judaism does not require the presence of a *minyan* for the recitation of *Kaddish* or any other prayer, it is appropriate that a *minyan* be assembled whenever possible. (Women are, of course, counted in the *minyan*.)

[129] There is no basis in Reform Judaism for the custom of reciting *Kaddish* for eleven months only (see the brief essay on *Kaddish* in the Appendix, p. 143).

[130] The term *yahrzeit* means literally "year's time," i.e., anniversary. The custom of *yahrzeit* is not mentioned in the Talmud or the medieval codes by that name. We find the word for the first time in the writings of a prominent fourteenth-century German talmudist, Rabbi Jacob Mölln (Maharil; see note 71). In talmudic times people followed the custom of a private fast day (*taanit yachid*) on the anniversary of the death of a parent (*Shevuot* 20a). The custom of burning a memorial lamp during the *yahrzeit* day originated in the Middle Ages and probably derives from the Christian custom of votive candles. By the nineteenth century it was a solid enough Jewish custom to be prescribed by Rabbi Solomon Ganzfried in his *Kitzur Shulchan Aruch*. (The Ganzfried passage on *yahrzeit* also makes explicit mention of the traditional belief that *Kaddish* and other *mitzvot* help the soul to ascend to higher spheres; see notes 124 and 127.)

The term *yahrzeit,* though Yiddish, is listed in the authoritative Israeli Hebrew dictionary, *Ha-Milon He-Hadash* (Even-Shoshan, Jerusalem, 1969) because of its common usage.

[131] *Yizkor* (lit. "May He remember") is the popular name of the special prayer prescribed in the liturgy for recitation on certain holy days, especially Yom Kippur, in memory of the dead. The custom of *hazkarat neshamot* (calling to mind the memory of the dead) is an ancient one, but the *Yizkor* prayer as recited in Ashkenazic congregations probably dates from after the Crusades. The Sefardic memorial prayer is known as *Hashkabah*. *Yizkor* is recited in all Reform congregations on Yom Kippur and the last day of Pesach and in many congregations on Shavuot and Atzeret–Simchat Torah also (see *Gates of Prayer*, pp. 546–53).

[132] It would be impossible to catalogue all the mourning customs that have been and are observed by different communities of Jews. The mourning period is one of great personal vulnerability, and mourners often take upon themselves customs that are not in keeping with their religious philosophies. Prominent among the customs that are not prescribed for Reform Jews are: entering the home after a funeral through the rear door, washing the hands outside the house, covering all mirrors and pictures, sitting on low stools or boxes, not wearing shoes, not shaving, and many others.

[133] The custom of erecting a monument (*matzevah*) over a grave is an ancient one (see Genesis 35:20 and II Samuel 18:18), but it did not become normative in Judaism until the Middle Ages. A great thirteenth-century Spanish authority, Rabbi Solomon Adret, prescribed the use of a *matzevah* as a way of honoring the dead. But much earlier tradition disagrees; "Rabbi Simeon ben Gamliel taught: 'We need not erect monuments for the righteous; their accomplishments are their memorials'" (Midrash, *Genesis Rabbah* 82:11).

FOUR ESSAYS ON *MITZVAH*

THE four essays on *mitzvah* that follow speak for themselves; they need no interpretation. Each was written by a rabbi and leader of the Reform movement to whom *mitzvah* is a way of life.

In introducing them, however, it is necessary to explain that Jewish tradition makes a distinction between *mitzvot bein adam la-Makom*—commandments between a person and God—and *mitzvot bein adam lachavero*—commandments between one person and another. The former category includes all those *mitzvot* related to the observance of Sabbaths, festivals, and the life cycle, i.e., the *ritual* aspects of Judaism; the latter includes such *mitzvot* as "You shall love your neighbor as yourself," "You shall not oppress the stranger," "The wages of an employee may not remain unpaid overnight," i.e., *ethics*.

Jewish tradition does not identify one *mitzvah* or one group of *mitzvot* as more important than another. The devout Jew observes both ethical and ritual *mitzvot*. In fact, it is often difficult to distinguish between the two. For example, what *mitzvah* could be more elaborately ritualistic than the Passover *Seder* with its myriad details? But the purpose of the *Seder* is to teach a supreme ethical principle: that God created us to be free. Is the observance of Passover, then, a ritual or an ethical *mitzvah*?

The purpose of this book, as stated in the Introduction, is "to help Jews make *Jewish* responses, to give their lives *Jewish* depth and character"; as such it deals primarily, though not exclusively, with ritual *mitzvot*. But recognizing that the laws of ethical conduct are basic to Judaism—or, as Rabbi Akiba said of "Love your neighbor": it is a *kelal gadol,* a supreme principle—Rabbi Arthur J. Lelyveld was invited to write an essay on *"Mitzvah:* The Larger Context." That "larger context," for Rabbi Lelyveld, is "action in the world in behalf of human rights, justice, and peace." To publish a book on the *mitzvot* of Judaism without some reference to its ethics would be unthinkable.

The essays of Rabbis Roland B. Gittelsohn, David Polish, and Herman E. Schaalman are concerned primarily with the source of the *mitzvot*. Each of them urgently prescribes the performance of *mitzvot* as a means of enriching one's personal and family life and contributing to the perpetuation of Judaism, but each comes to that urgency from a different place. Each suggests that a *mitzvah*—commandment—must derive from a *metzaveh*—commander, but each defines that *metzaveh* differently.

Rabbi Schaalman hears the voice of the commanding God as the *metzaveh* behind each *mitzvah;* "it all depends on whether I am ready to live my life in relationship to God, in response to Him, in my acceptance of His being Commander and of me as His covenant partner . . ." Rabbi Polish apprehends the *mitzvot* through the history and shared experience of the Jewish people: "When a Jew performs one of the many life-acts known as *mitzvot* . . . what was only a moment in Jewish history becomes eternal in Jewish life."

Rabbi Gittelsohn's essay is shorter than the others and is actually a naturalist commentary on the Schaalman and Polish essays and should be read along with them. Gittelsohn, too, posits a *metzaveh* as the source of *mitzvot* and speaks of historic encounters between this *metzaveh* and the Jewish people, but he defines the *metzaveh* as "the Spiritual Energy, Essence, Core, or Thrust of the universe, not a discrete Supernatural Being."

Rabbis Gittelsohn, Lelyveld, and Schaalman wrote their essays for this book; Rabbi Polish's essay is a reworking of the introductory essays that he wrote along with Rabbi Frederic A. Doppelt for *A Guide for Reform Jews* (New York, 1957). The inclusion of the Polish essay serves as a tribute, not only to the authors of that pioneering attempt to bring Reform Jews to lives consecrated by *mitzvot*, but to all those rabbis who have written guides for their congregations or for wider Jewish audiences. Many of these works were consulted in the preparation of this volume; we are grateful to all those colleagues who worked so diligently "that you may remember and do all My commandments, and be holy to your God" (Numbers 15:40).

While the four essayists come to *mitzvot* from different directions, all would agree that a Jewish life devoid of *mitzvot* is a pale shadow of what it might be and that *mitzvot* "represent the difference between talking or philosophizing about Judaism and *living* it." Some readers will prefer one approach; some will prefer another. Such diversity of views is not new in Judaism. "For three years there was a dispute between the Schools of Shammai and of Hillel. Then a heavenly voice proclaimed: *Both are the words of the living God!*" (Talmud J., *Berachot* 1:7).

THE DIVINE AUTHORITY

OF THE *MITZVAH*

Herman E. Schaalman

WHY should I perform *mitzvot*? What does it mean to say: "A commandment, a *mitzvah*, has been given to me?" Who commands? Who has the authority to summon me to do or not to do a given thing, sometimes even at a given time?

Some would say: "This is our tradition, the Jewish way." And while, obviously, some are satisfied thus to accept this tradition and, more or less unquestioningly, to insert themselves into its chain, others will ask: "Who started this tradition? Who first accepted the *mitzvot*? How did it all begin?"

Some might answer these questions by explaining that *mitzvot* are the peculiar way by which the Jewish people created and expressed its specific, unique style of life. In this view the *mitzvot* are the customs, the laws, the directives, which Jews have formulated from the beginning in much the same way that similar religious folkways appear in other cultures and among other groups. According to this view, the authority of the "commandment" resides in the *people*. As long as I am a member of my people, as long as I identify as a Jew, the "commandments" of my people apply to me and are the most obvious and effective demonstration of my belonging, of my identity as a Jew.

Were the Jews a people like any other people, then this would be a sufficient, a good answer. What is puzzling, though, is that these "customs" and "folkways" are called *mitzvot*, commandments. The Hebrew vocabulary is rich in terms which could have said it in other ways. There are terms such as *minhag*, "custom," or *derech eretz*, "the way things are done," and others. Why would the Jewish people have chosen the term *mitzvah*?

The word, as well as the history of our people as stated in the Torah, points to a different answer. A *mitzvah*—commandment—comes from a *Metzaveh*, a Commander. In our case, indisputably, that Commander was God, first by way of Moses and then by way of prophets and rabbis, the spiritual descendants of Moses.

Of course, this answer immediately raises a host of other questions. What do we mean by stating that God is Commander, *Metzaveh?* How does God command? Does he "speak"? How did Moses or others "hear"? Why *these* commandments as found in Torah and later tradition and not others?

Revelation, for that is what we are talking about, is a mystery. The character of a mystery, its very essence, precludes our ability to describe and analyze it with precision, in clearly stated detail. If we could so understand and describe it, it would no longer be a mystery. There is something impenetrable about a mystery, something that ultimately defies our human efforts at understanding in ordinary, day-to-day terms.

And yet, at the same time, we are fascinated and almost compelled to say something about it. And so we use ordinary, everyday words to hint at the impenetrable, to point toward, though never define, the mystery. And then we say: "God speaks" and "man hears."

We should not forget, though sometimes we do, that we use the phrases "God speaks" and "man hears" in an approximate, vague, allusive, and nondefinitive way. Only when we forget are we misled into thinking that God speaks as we do (what language? Hebrew?) and that those who hear God do so as we hear each other (are there sound waves coming from God?).

Language is the problem here. We use terms such as *speaks* and *hears* when talking of God in the same manner as we do when talking of humans. We apply them to the mystery of encounter with God, to the unique and rare moments when a given person and the Divine Presence "meet," without making due allowance for the essentially different use and meaning of these words when they are applied to the mystery of revelation.

God becomes the "Speaker," the "Commander," the *Metzaveh,* because Moses, in his extraordinary nearness to Him, thus understood, thus interpreted, thus "heard," the impact and meaning of God's Presence. God is

Metzaveh—Commander—because Moses experienced himself as *metzuveh* —commanded, summoned, directed. And this is why Moses transmitted what he "heard," why he expressed the meaning of God's Presence in the *mitzvot*, the commandments to the people at Sinai and to their descendants ever after. This is why the Torah is both *Torat Adonai*, God's Torah, and *Torat Mosheh*, Moses' Torah.

This is why the Talmud can say: "*Dibra Torah bilshon benei adam*— Torah speaks human language." Hebrew is a human language, like all languages. Torah, both written and oral, is a collection of human documents flowing out of the encounter of God and man, flowing out of the mystery of revelation. Torah is the recording by men in their language, their concepts, their ability to express and to articulate, what God's "coming down" (Exodus 19:20), His making Himself present, means.

Why do we do *mitzvot*? Why should we do *mitzvot*? Because we are the descendants of those ancestors, the children of those parents who said at Sinai: "*Na-aseh ve-nishma*—We shall do and we shall hear" (Exodus 24:7). All authentic Judaism until now has so understood itself, has so acted and so handed it on to hitherto faithful new generations. Thus the Divine Presence waits for us, and we for It. Thus the commandment comes to us in our time, asking to be heard, understood, and done.

Wouldn't we, then, have to do all of them? Why do non-Orthodox Jews not keep all the *mitzvot*? What entitles anyone to make selections? First off, no one, not even the most meticulous and strictly observant Jew, keeps "all" of the *mitzvot* as found in the written and oral Torah. Traditional Jewish authority, after the destruction of the Temple and the Diaspora, declared major categories of *mitzvot* to be inoperative. The scope of commandments, even for the most traditional Jews, has shrunk, for all practical purposes, to *mitzvot* concerning worship, learning, family life, *kashrut*, acts of human concern, etc. But even within this shrunken perimeter, there is room for variant interpretations, even disagreement and conflicting opinions. This is one of the characteristics and undoubted virtues of the Jewish life style.

It is built into the very definition and basic assumption of a *mitzvah* that it is the human response to the "Commanding Presence of God." That response is not, and cannot be, invariably the same. It depends on circumstances. It is not automatic. That response to the commanding God should never be altogether unthinking, routine. To be a genuine response of the person to God, it needs to take account of the condition, capacity, responsiveness, of the commanded one, i.e., me. I cannot respond like an automaton, every time the same way. Nor should I be expected to. I must make my response freely, "with all my heart, all my soul, all my might" (Deuteronomy 4:29). This means, surely, that I should not be negligent or devoted only to self-gratification. Such an attitude would surely indicate unwillingness to be "commanded." It would signify my withdrawal from *mitzvah* and from the *Metzaveh*, the commanding God.

To be commanded—to "listen and do"—must engage me, the doer, as what I am and can do and will do at the moment when the *mitzvah* confronts me or I seek it. There are times when I cannot or will not do the commandment, and I will know it and bear the consequences, perhaps standing in need of *teshuvah*, repentance. And there will be *mitzvot* through which my forebears found themselves capable of responding to the commanding God which are no longer adequate or possible for me, just as there will be new *mitzvot* through which I or my generation will be able to respond which my ancestors never thought of.

Finally it all depends or whether I am ready to live my life in relationship to God, in response to Him, in my acceptance of His being Commander and of me as His covenant partner, giving life to the *berit*—the covenant—by my *mitzvah* response. And while I have and retain the freedom of choosing my specific means of response at a given moment, the essential fact of my life will be my intention to respond. And once my feet are set on this road, then even what at one time appears opaque and incapable of eliciting my response may do so at another time. The number of *mitzvot* I thus choose to perform is not nearly as important as is the fullness of my awareness and intention, for it is likely that in time I may hear the authentic "voice of God" in many more *mitzvot* than at first I could have imagined.

The difficult, the decisive, step is the first one, to place oneself into the covenant with the Commanding God. Thereafter, one's own integrity and the joy of fulfillment will move him along the way. The important step is the first one. Therefore, begin!

HISTORY AS

THE SOURCE OF THE *MITZVAH*

David Polish

THE observance of *mitzvot* reflects a Jewish conception of history. This conception is composed of two elements. The first consists of historical events of which we are reminded by specific practices. The second consists of an outlook upon human events and the world which is embodied in a system of conduct and discipline, individual as well as corporate.

Mitzvot are related to historic experiences in which the Jewish people sought to apprehend God's nature and His will. They are to be observed not because they are divine fiats, but because something happened between God and Israel, and the same something continues to happen in every age and land. Note the words of blessing preceding the performance of a *mitzvah*: "*asher kideshanu be-mitzvotav, ve-tzivanu . . .* who has sanctified us by His *mitzvot* and has commanded us . . ." *Mitzvot* sanctify the Jewish people because they mark points of encounter by the Jewish people with God. They are enjoined upon us, because through them we perpetuate memories of the encounters and are sustained by those memories. Since they are so indigenous to us, they are incumbent primarily upon us, the Jewish people, and they constitute the singularity of the Jewish religion.

Mitzvot thus emerge from the womb of Jewish history, from a series of sacred encounters between God and Israel. When a Jew performs one of the many life-acts known as *mitzvot* to remind himself of one of those moments of encounter, what was only episodic becomes epochal, and what was only a moment in Jewish history becomes eternal in Jewish life.

Mitzvot are rooted in the biblical declaration: "It is a sign between Me

A more complete development of Rabbi Polish's concept of *mitzvah* can be found in *A Guide for Reform Jews* by F. Doppelt and D. Polish (New York, 1957), pp. 12–27.

and the children of Israel forever" (Exodus 31:17). *Mitzvot* are "signs" of the covenant, affirmed and reaffirmed through the ages at various turning-points in which Jewish existence stood in the balance. Out of these turning-points came hallowed insights, pointing to the pivotal moment and fashioning the *mitzvah* marking it. Thus, the Chanukah lights, marking Israel's rededication after near-extinction. Thus, *milah* (circumcision), which began with Abraham and which was invoked with special intensity during critical periods in Jewish history.

Moments in the life of the individual Jew are intimately related to Israel's historic career. To be sure, they are infused with the most intense kind of personal meaning, but they are at the same time bound up with the experiences of the people. Thus the *mitzvot* around birth, *milah*, naming, education, marriage, and death take on added meaning because in each case the individual is made conscious of his own role in Jewish history. *Milah* renews the covenant into which the individual enters with God and with all the generations of Israel who have been committed to a specific historical destiny. It is into that covenant-relationship that the Jew of every generation reenters when he personally participates in the *mitzvah* of *milah*. The *berit milah* service says it quite clearly: ". . . to bring him into the covenant of our father Abraham." The same principle applies to the *mitzvah* of eating *matzah* on Pesach. It marks the encounter of our people with the God of freedom at the turning-point in our history when we broke the shackles of Egyptian bondage. And it makes us sensitive to the modern bondages of which Egypt is a paradigm.

Jewish observance depends upon the triune and inextricable encounter of Israel with God, Israel with the world, and Israel with its own destiny, and from this encounter it derives its meaning. It is the cryptic symbolism whereby we relive Jewish history and contribute to its continuity. This symbolism is predicated upon the summons to Israel to remember—to remember the roots of its being. The call to remembrance—*zachor, ve-zacharta*—is as vehement and as consistent as any other imperative evoked by the Bible. Thus the *Kiddush* for Shabbat and the festivals makes its demand upon our memories of the Exodus.

Kedushah (sanctity) and *mitzvah* are vital components of this historical perception. Without them Jewish observance can have no real meaning. In the indispensable rubric *asher ḳideshanu be-mitzvotav* are embodied the awareness of the inherent sanctity of Jewish existence and the divine imperative under which Jews live and to which they are subject. It is surely significant that so many Jewish observances are called by derivatives of the word *ḳadosh—Kiddush, Kaddish, Kiddushin, Kedushah*, and God Himself is referred to as *Ha-Kadosh baruch Hu*, the Holy One, blessed be He.

It cannot be stressed too strongly that the observance of any particular *mitzvah* is a symbol of, and points to, a higher truth. Some symbols, because of their overpowering hold on us, endure; others change. Some fall into desuetude; new ones come into being. Thus, there is bound to emerge a compelling symbolism and observance which will someday speak to our people of the twin events of twentieth-century Judaism: the Holocaust and the establishment of Israel—catastrophe and rebirth. This new symbolism will capture the essential meaning of those events, a meaning which is fraught with the very elements which informed the Exodus and every one of its counterparts in our history—the presence of God in history, the struggle by Israel to preserve its being, and the confrontation of Israel with the world.

Jewish observance also reflects Judaism's moral verdict on history, a verdict which is hopeful, but also implacable in its redemptive expectations within history. This attitude and its counterpart are reflected in the second era of Christian-Jewish history. In 410 Rome was sacked by the Goths. At about the same time, the Jerusalem Talmud was completed and the Patriarchate came to an end. Each of these turning-points represented a challenge and a response which Christianity and Judaism faced and dealt with in disparate ways. Christianity responded with Augustine's "City of God," which attempts to interpret history in terms of negation. Judaism responded by establishing a panoramic code of living within the structure of society and this life.

Augustine's view of society is predicated upon man's sinful and corrupt nature, from which there can be no earthly escape. The talmudic response to the challenge of adversity is conscious of social corruption. Yet it is essentially resistant and pragmatic, and it is symbolized in a complex regimen of conduct. The regimen may no longer fully minister to our needs, but its underlying affirmation, that the incursions of evil in the world are to be met by a strategy of collective moral discipline and conduct, is as valid today as ever. The self-imposed discipline of observance, to which the Jew submits as a sacred *mitzvah*, thus becomes a symbol of the commitment of his faith and of his people to the unending struggle to enthrone God in the world within the bounds of human history. It is also a sign of the Jew's commitment to the covenant, which each generation renews, and which each Jew reenacts in the regimen of Jewish living. By this discipline he not only renews the covenant, but he *chooses* to renew it. He transcends time and stands with Abraham and with our ancestors at Sinai, to play his part in helping to perfect the world under the kingdom of God.

Finally, the *mitzvah* enabled the Jewish people to live creatively in cataclysmic times. *Mitzvah* was the defiant response of the Jew to efforts at crushing his spirit. It helped preserve him as a person and it helped preserve the people. Together with all humanity, we are moving through apocalyptic times which may additionally test not only our people's *capacity* to endure but our *will* to endure as Jews. It would be an overstatement to say that *mitzvot* will guarantee our survival, but it can be said that our individual and collective decision to persist as Jews will be aided by cultivating a life of *mitzvot*.

Because of the apocalyptic nature of our times, *mitzvot* will also strengthen the Jew's resolve to retain his humanity and his moral strength when the foundations of the world are shaking. Many of the certainties of the past are shattered. The very future of civilization has become problematic. *Mitzvot* are our link with antiquity and eternity, both of which have enabled us to survive apocalypse before. We are called upon to be in the world. *Mitzvot* enable us momentarily to transcend the world and, strengthened, to return to it as we must.

MITZVAH WITHOUT MIRACLES

Roland B. Gittelsohn

W HAT can *mitzvah* mean to a modern Jew who is a religious naturalist? Perhaps a prior question should be: what is a religious naturalist? Briefly, he or she is a person who believes in God, but asserts that God inheres within nature and operates through natural law. A religious naturalist perceives God to be the Spiritual Energy, Essence, Core, or Thrust of the universe, not a discrete Supernatural Being.

What, then, can *mitzvah* mean to such an individual? Certainly more than custom or folkway, more than social covenant or mores. *Mitzvah*, by very definition, must be cosmically grounded; it must possess empyreal significance. For the religious naturalist, as for all believing, practicing Jews, in order to have *mitzvah*—that which has been commanded—there must be a *metzaveh*, a commander. That commander, moreover, needs to be more than human ingenuity or convenience.

In the mainstream of Jewish tradition through the centuries, this posed no great problem. The *metzaveh* was God. A *mitzvah* was God's will. It had to be performed because God wanted it. It may have made sense to the human mind or not; these things were not important. It had to be done, plainly and simply, because God had commanded it.

But how can an Energy or Essence, a Core or a Thrust, command? For the religious naturalist, who is the *metzaveh*? Answer: reality itself. Or, more precisely, the physical and spiritual laws which govern reality. *Mitzvot* must be observed because only by recognizing and conforming to the nature of their environment can human beings increase the probability of their survival in any meaningful way. *Mitzvot* are not man-made; they inhere within the universe. Our Jewish mystics suspected this long ago. Mordecai Kaplan has summarized the view of the *Zohar* as holding that "*mitzvot* are part of the very process whereby the world came into being."

I agree with David Polish (see p. 104) that *mitzvot* are binding upon us "because something happened between God and Israel, and the same something continues to happen in every land and age." What makes me a religious naturalist is interpreting the "something" to be a historic encounter between the Jewish people and the highest Spiritual Reality human beings have ever known or felt. No other people has been so persistent as ours in seeking that Reality and its moral imperatives.

It is easy to illustrate the cosmic nature of *mitzvot* on the level of physical reality. The universe is so constructed that, if I wish to survive, I must have adequate oxygen, nourishment, and exercise. God "wants" me to breathe fresh air, ingest healthful foods, and regularly move my muscles. These, therefore, are *mitzvot*.

No less is true in the realm of ethical *mitzvot*. Honesty is a compelling *mitzvah*. Human nature (which is, after all, nature at its highest level of development) is such that in the long run the individual or the social group that consistently flaunts the dictates of honesty risks disaster. The struggle for freedom is a compelling *mitzvah*. Ultimately only those who cherish their own freedom and grant it to others can achieve happiness. To love is a compelling *mitzvah*. Only the person who is capable of giving and receiving love will ever be fulfilled. These things are true, not because we want them to be and not because they were decreed by a human legislature, but because they are ineluctable aspects of reality. Hence the recognition, acceptance, and observance of them constitute *mitzvot*.

Most of the *mitzvot* spelled out in this guide, however, deal with ritual observance rather than physical law or ethics. Are they, too, related to cosmic reality? In a less obvious but equally binding sense than the physical or moral imperatives suggested above, yes. Human nature is such that we need to express our emotions and ideals with our whole bodies, not just our tongues. We need also to be visually and kinetically reminded of our noblest values and stimulated to pursue them. As otherwise lonely and frightened individuals, we need common practices and observances which bind us into meaningful and supportive groups. All of which adds up to the fact that we need ritual as something more than social luxury or convenience. For us as Reform Jews, a particular ritual may not be *mitzvah*. But the need for a pattern of such rituals, this—because it grows out of and satisfies our very basic nature as human beings—is *mitzvah*. And this we desperately need.

A concrete example at this point may be more instructive than further paragraphs of theoretical exposition. The most elaborate—and perhaps the most valuable—*mitzvah* in our tradition is the *seder* ceremony. A supernaturalistically oriented Jew celebrates at his *seder* God's miraculous intervention in nature and history.

The *seder* means no less, however, to the religiously naturalistic Jew, who rejects miracles. Plugging into centuries of his people's tradition as well as its unique pursuit of freedom, he visually, audibly, and dramatically commemorates that pursuit and rededicates himself to it. His *metzaveh* is triune: his very special human need to be free, both as a person and a Jew; his equally human need to augment speech with memory and motion in reinforcement of his highest values; and his specifically Jewish need to identify with his people's destiny.

Permeating our theological differences is the common understanding that God, however divergently we interpret Him, is the Core Spiritual Essence of reality. In this sense, God is the *metzaveh* of the religiously naturalistic Jew, who eschews the supernatural not only in theological speculation but also in his approach to *mitzvot*. He responds naturalistically to his own essence and to that of his universal setting. *Mitzvot* for him represent the difference between talking or philosophizing about Judaism and *living* it. They bind him firmly, visibly, to his people and his tradition. They speak to him imperatively because he is Jewish and wants to remain so.

MITZVAH:

THE LARGER CONTEXT

Arthur J. Lelyveld

THE word *mitzvah* has been used by Jews for thousands of years with different levels of meaning, ranging all the way from the broad ethical injunction "You shall be holy for I, the Lord your God, am Holy" to what in popular usage is a simple good deed: "Please go see your grandmother; it would be a *mitzvah*." But there is a core of steel in the word when used in its classic sense that is not there when it is used to mean an act of benevolence or a simple ritual act. The word *Mitzvah*, writ large and uttered reverently, means an act which I perform because God requires it of me.

The different levels of usage of the word *mitzvah* pose a problem for the liberal Jew who takes his Judaism seriously. In the view of our Orthodox brethren, God demands the fulfillment of all the commandments, both negative and positive, as recorded in the Torah and as seen through the spectrum of the oral tradition and its development down through the ages. For the strictly traditional Jew, the Talmud and the great medieval codes, as interpreted by authoritative rabbinic scholars, define what a Jew is expected to do. From the moment he opens his eyes in the morning to the moment he closes them at night, and to the moment that he closes them on his deathbed, his conduct is prescribed. But how do we liberals discern the divine demand? How do we train ourselves to respond with *mitzvah* (the deed) to *mitzvah* (the demand)?

We liberal Jews read Scripture not as the literal word of God, but as the work of members of the people of Israel seeking to *understand* the demand of God. Once we approach our Bible within that frame of reference, we necessarily become selective, for there are points in Scripture at which man has broken through to an understanding of the highest, while there are also points that preserve primitive practices, anachronisms, or injunctions that long ago became obsolete.

The solution of our difficulty lies in the very fact that we use the word *mitzvah* in two distinct ways. We talk about specific *mitzvot*, and we also speak of *Mitzvah* in a more generalized sense, as enjoining upon us a certain attitude toward our fellows. Abraham Heschel makes clear this comprehensive meaning of *mitzvah* when he quotes Rabbi Nachman of Bratzlav, the great Chassidic sage, as having said, "Every act done in agreement with the will of God is *mitzvah*"; and George Foot Moore, the great Christian expert on the thinking of our rabbis of the first and second centuries, says that the word *mitzvah* is most frequently used as meaning not a specific commandment, but any *particular* opportunity "to fulfill the comprehensive duty of man to his fellowman." Thus to do a *mitzvah* is to act in accord with God's will, in accord with God's demand upon mankind.

From this point of view, our liberal picking and choosing among the *mitzvot* makes sense. We are bidden to ask the questions, "When does God speak to us? When does God make demands upon us?" In the answers to these questions we may find the larger *Mitzvot—Mitzvah* written here with a capital *M*.

Small-*m mitzvot*—the performance of ritual acts—have an aesthetic and affective function. They both beautify and enhance by religious drama the moral values and the ideals of our heritage. They become a structure on which the preservation of our people's tradition and its continuity may rest. We select the *mitzvot* we will perform, we shape our folkways, change our music, revise our prayers, eliminate customs and add other and new customs. But *Mitzvah* is not the product of our human social engineering. *Mitzvah* is God's demand issuing in moral and spiritual values. Ceremonial *mitzvot* with their folk associations, their customs, and their symbolic objects and actions are the carrier of the values, the structural framework for the people's task of transmission. But large-*M Mitzvah* is the enduring essence to which the structure of small *m* testifies and pays obeisance.

This is a distinction made by the prophets of Israel as far back as the eighth century before the common era. When Amos proclaimed the words, "I hate, I despise your feasts . . . but let justice well up as waters and righteousness as a mighty stream," he was making a distinction between formal adherence to practices of ritual observance and the response to the great Demand of God. When Isaiah cried out, "To what purpose is the multitude of your sacrifices unto Me? . . . Who asked you to trample My courts? . . . Cease to do evil, learn to do well, seek justice, relieve the oppressed," and when Micah summarized God's demand, "Wherewith shall I come back before the Lord and bow before God on high? Will the Lord be pleased with thousands of rams or with . . . rivers of oil? . . . You have been told, O man, what is good and what the Lord requires of you: only to do justly and to love mercy and to walk humbly with your God," they were seeking the inner meaning of *Mitzvah*, the demand of God.

Contemporary, secular value-philosophy also supports this distinction when it recognizes the essential relationship between value and the enduring Demand to which we must bring a commitment. Henry Margenau tells us (*New Knowledge in Human Values,* ed. Abraham Maslow, 1959) that values are arbitrary choices unless they are related to "command." For example, life has no "value" to a person who is earnestly committed to its destruction, as in war. But Margenau says, "If you are committed to the prior maxim expressed in the Decalogue, *Thou shalt not kill,* then the value of life follows as a theorem follows from a postulate."

So it is with honesty, veracity, friendship, love of mankind, and every other ideal. They receive their "value" from a command, a directive to which the individual is committed. In other words, there can be no structure of values or of moral choice without *Mitzvah*.

In the last analysis, liberalism cannot escape its commitment to the supreme right and obligation of decision which is reserved to the individual soul. It is true that this makes the individual the ultimate authority as to what is *Mitzvah* and what is not *Mitzvah*. "I must distinguish in my innermost being between what is commanded me and what is not commanded me," says Martin Buber. But the awesomeness of this existential responsibility is mitigated for the Jew by the fact that he stands in the midst of a covenant community and that he is bidden to hear the *Mitzvah* as an informed and committed individual within the informed and committed community.

Mitzvah, therefore, speaks differently to us than it did to our great-

great-grandfathers. Cut off from the larger world, they retained the ideal of mankind's ultimate perfection, in their liturgy, in their aspirations, and in their obligation under the covenant *le-takein olam*—to perfect the world. The only task that was within their capacity as Jews was to be faithful, to observe 613 *mitzvot* and to practice *kiddush ha-chayim,* the effort to make the Divine Presence felt in the world. But the quarrels among kings and princes, the violence and the cruelty, the servitude of the peasants, were all part of the world of the gentiles. Even when our forebears recognized that the most stringent troubles were the troubles that affected *both* Israel and the world, they could not but feel that the only action required of them was personal witness and prayer.

We, in contrast to these ancestors, are part of the larger world. This is the precious and unhappy result of emancipation. We are participant, in destiny and in responsibility, with all men. We cannot even pretend to be building God's Kingdom by the faithful witness of personal discipline. For us, the demand of God which challenges us to compassion and to respect for the divine image in every fellowman must as *Mitzvah* eventuate in the *Mitzvah* which is performance: action in the world in behalf of human rights, justice, and peace.

This conception of the role of *Mitzvah* is not alien to our tradition. The Midrash tells us that "the *mitzvot* were given to Israel in order to purify mankind" (*Leviticus Rabbah* 13:3). These particular and specific commands were given for a universal purpose—the perfection of *all* human beings. When we understand *Mitzvah* in this sense, we can begin to say what is expected of the modern Jew. We are entitled to expect that he will act, that he will perform the *Mitzvah*, in response to the divine *Mitzvah*—the deed in response to the demand—and that he will do so as a Jew within the context of the three-thousand-year experience of his people.

The ancient aphorism that tells us what it is that sustains the entire world also tells us how to be a Jew today. "The world stands upon three things: *Torah*, study; *avodah*, worship; and *gemilut chasadim*, deeds of lovingkindness." Under these three categories we can still bracket the primary *Mitzvot* and what a Jew must *do*.

Torah means that he will become part of the three-thousand-year experience that shaped our Jewish value-stance, by studying with his people, by devoting some part of his time to continuous Jewish learning. This is the foundation.

Avodah means that he will refine his sense of his people's aspirations by worshipping with the community, by practicing joyfully the richest of its distinctive mores: the *simchah* of Sukkot, the pride of Chanukah, the avowal of freedom in Pesach, the acceptance of the Torah and the covenant in Shavuot, and the weekly rededication and purification of soul in the Sabbath.

Gemilut chasadim means that the Jew will concern himself with the needs of others, of his people and of his world. This response of loving-kindness is commanded and is *Mitzvah*. The traditional *mitzvot* of hospitality, concern for the sick and the bereaved, and the demand that we meet the human needs of the dispossessed are all fragments of the *Mitzvah* of *gemilut chasadim*.

The Jew must *act*. The Ten Commandments are not enough. As real Jews, we must actively love our neighbor, seek justice, and struggle against those practices and prejudices that stifle the image of God in man. These, as Leviticus 19 clearly shows, are the ways in which we demonstrate that we are *kedoshim*, reflections of the Divine presentness.

Appendix

The following brief essays
and the Glossary were written by members of
the Committee on Reform Jewish Practice
(except as indicated).

THE SINGLE PERSON,

THE SINGLE-PARENT FAMILY

AND *MITZVOT*

> It is a *mitzvah* for the family to gather together and con-
> secrate the Shabbat and festival table . . .
> It is a *mitzvah* to have guests at one's table, especially
> for the celebration of Shabbat and festivals.
> "Marriage and the Jewish Home," *E–8 and E–10*

FEW comprehend the centrality of marriage and family in Judaism so
poignantly as Jewish singles and their children. Intact families usually
experience traditional life-cycle and holiday *mitzvot* as affirmations of
their familial identity. In single-parent families and among singles, however, traditional rituals often compound the loneliness and emphasize
the deviance from the Jewish norm. Jewish observances frequently remind
the divorced of their shattered dreams of *shelom bayit*, family harmony.
A child's wedding may force still-warring parents into painful coexistence
and reunion with former in-laws. The widowed and their orphaned
children mourn especially during rituals in which the dead parent would
have participated, such as a *Bar Mitzvah* or Passover *seder*.

On the other hand, traditional Jewish observances provide unique
opportunities for the individual's and family's assertion of their continued existence despite tragedy. When single-parent families celebrate
the Shabbat rituals designed for intact families, they bind themselves
together in renewed support for each other and with more certain convic-
tion of their survival. When a *Bar Mitzvah* boy can acknowledge his
longing for his dead father or mother on the day of his first *aliyah*, he
transcends his tragedy on a level unattainable in the absence of Jewish
observance.

For the Jewish single or single-parent family, traditional ritual en-
genders more difficulty than for the intact family. Necessary preparations
for Shabbat and holidays, in the midst of already overburdened schedules,

complicate their observance. However, performance of *mitzvot* despite adversity produces special satisfaction. The single parent who prepares Shabbat dinner after an exhausting week of office work, child rearing, and housework, may understand Shabbat *menuchah* (Sabbath rest) on a particularly profound level.

Single Jews may enhance Jewish observance and overcome many of its emotional and practical obstacles through *chavurot* (voluntary fellowships for the study and practice of Judaism) of singles or single-parent families. Joining others for Shabbat dinner lessens the difficulty of preparation. Sharing holidays in a *chavurah* decreases the loneliness and the feeling of alienation from other Jews.

Intact couples and families may at first feel awkward inviting singles and single-parent families to participate in Jewish observances with them. However, the *mitzvah* of *hachnasat orchim* (hospitality) suggests that no holiday or Shabbat observance is complete without such guests. The biblical instructions to care for the orphan and the widow extend to never-married and divorced adults and to fatherless or motherless children as well. Every temple and every Jewish family should fulfill the *mitzvah* of assisting victims of family tragedy to continue their synagogue memberships, their children's Jewish educations, and their full participation in the temple and in home ritual.

Life-cycle observances, such as *Bar* or *Bat Mitzvah* and weddings, constitute awkward situations for single-parent families. Unless the participants confront the feelings of parents and children with candor and appropriate caution, the tragedies of the past can undermine the *simchah* (joy) of the present. If the pain of the past is acknowledged, the various aspects of the celebration discussed with all participants, and the involvement of each adult and each child considered, the observance can be a source of new strength and increased maturity for all involved.

Although widows and widowers frequently hesitate to discuss the memory of the dead spouse in preparation for a life-cycle observance, such suppression of memory is contrary to the Jewish tradition and to the insights of psychology as well. The experience of many indicates that appropriate acknowledgment of the tragedies of the past can lead to a richer appreciation of the present.

Ignoring the bride's sadness that her dead father will not be able to accompany her down the aisle may undermine the wedding for her. Similarly, the involvement of divorced parents in a *Bar Mitzvah* should be discussed with the rabbi and handled with caution and sensitivity. Variation in ritual or custom in such cases can add immeasurably to the meaning of the observance.

The needs of the Jewish single and single-parent family are becoming an increasingly important concern in the Jewish community. Jews marry at a later age than members of most other groups. The Jewish divorce rate approximates that of the surrounding society. Cancer, heart disease, and accident leave many adults widowed and many children with only one living parent. Longer life expectancy sometimes means that one spouse may outlive the other by decades of loneliness. Although singleness may complicate the usual patterns of Jewish observance, the traditional rituals remain resources of potential strength for Jewish singles and their families.

—Mark L. Winer

＊ ＊

TZEDAKAH

It is a *mitzvah* to make a gift of *tzedakah* in honor of the birth of one's child.

"Birth, Childhood, and Education," *A–6*

THE above quotation from the first section of this book refers to one of the occasions in the Jewish life cycle when it is appropriate to give *tzedakah*. There are similar references in the sections on "Marriage and the Jewish Home" (C-7 and E-5) and "Death and Mourning" (C-6 and D-16) indicating that it is a *mitzvah* to contribute to worthy institutions in honor or in memory of loved ones.

The term *tzedakah* is derived from the Hebrew root *tzedek*, meaning "justice" or "righteousness," as found, for example, in Deuteronomy 16:20: "*Tzedek tzedek tirdof*—Justice, justice you shall pursue." *Tzedek* in this context refers to ethical and moral dealings with fellow human beings, whether in the areas of business, family life, the courts, or government. The concept of *tzedakah* as a form of charity is an extension of the original concept of *tzedek* as justice and righteousness, so that the term *tzedakah* has been translated as "righteous giving."

According to the Torah and subsequent Jewish law, every Jew is obligated to extend a helping hand to a person in need, Jew or non-Jew, and it is the inherent right of every person to be helped, "for there will never cease to be needy ones in your land, which is why I command you: open your hand to the poor and needy kinsman in your land" (Deuteronomy 15:11).

The underlying Jewish philosophy is that "the earth is the Lord's and all its fullness" (Psalms 24:1). Since everything belongs to God, we are merely the stewards of His infinite blessings, and it is, therefore, incumbent upon us—i.e., it is a *mitzvah*—to share His substance with others who are in need. This idea is spelled out succinctly in the harvest laws in Leviticus 19:9–10, where the landowner is commanded to leave the edges of his fields and the gleanings for the poor. They are entitled to a part of the harvest by sacred right; this is not *charity*—a gift of love (from the Latin *caritas*)—but *tzedakah*, an act of justice. One abuses the concept of *tzedek* if one does not share God-given bounty with the poor.

According to Maimonides (*Yad, Matnot Aniyim* 10:7–14), there are eight rungs on the ladder of *tzedakah*. The lowest is to give reluctantly, but the highest is to help a needy person to rehabilitate himself by extending a loan or by finding him suitable employment so that it will not be necessary for him to accept *tzedakah*.

Tzedakah is, of course, not restricted to direct help to the poor, though that is certainly its most crucial application. *Tzedakah* may also take the form of gifts to institutions, such as schools, hospitals, or worthy social welfare organizations in one's own community—Jewish or non-Jewish—or in Israel. And further, while *tzedakah* which serves the immediate physical needs of fellow human beings is a *mitzvah* of the greatest urgency, this is not the sole application of the *mitzvah*. There is *tzedakah* to the body and *tzedakah* to the soul. In the latter category would be gifts to cultural institutions which raise the general standard of living, e.g., synagogues, libraries, museums, civil liberties and environmental organizations, etc.

All of these are *tzedakah* if they are done in the spirit of justice, i.e., recognizing one's obligation as a human being to share one's bounty with the needy person and the community. And both the joyous and the sad occasions of the life cycle provide us with sacred opportunities for *tzedakah*.

＊ ＊

KIDDUSHIN

A JEWISH VIEW OF MARRIAGE

> It is a *mitzvah* for a Jew to marry and to live together with his/her spouse in a manner worthy of the traditional Hebrew designation for marriage, *Kiddushin* . . .
>
> "Marriage and the Jewish Home," *A–1*

NOTHING clarifies the Jewish attitude toward marriage quite as well as the traditional name for the wedding ceremony, *Kiddushin*, derived from the Hebrew *kadosh*—holy. As we come to understand the deeper meaning of *kadosh*, we may begin to appreciate why Jewish tradition reserved the word *Kiddushin* for marriage.

In the outlook of Judaism, all existence is derived originally from God and is, therefore, potentially holy. Time and space, God-given, are sacred but can also be desecrated by idolatry—the worship of things or of self. In consequence, we set special times and places aside for respect, for reverence, so that they may be kept apart from the realm of the profane, from exploitation for material gain and utilitarian usage. In time, the Sabbath; in space, the synagogues are instances which come to mind.* The prayer in which we set aside the Shabbat *day*, a time of value in and of itself and not for further gain or use, we call *Kiddush,* sanctification.

---

* The Talmud (*Megillah* 28a, cf. also 27b) teaches that one may not use the space of a house of worship as a thoroughfare or shortcut from one place outside the sanctuary to another. One must, in respect, go around the hallowed space.

Humanity lives, however, not only in the dimensions of time and space, but also, from birth, in the dimension of relationship. And while all relationships, like all time and space, should be considered essentially sacred, certain relationships are especially exalted. In Judaism the Holy of Holies of all relationships, to which the poetic genius of the Hebraic spirit turned most often for the paradigm of the covenant between God and Israel, was and is the covenant between husband and wife (see, for example, Hosea 1 and 2). A sacred entity comes into being in Jewish marriage. As in the *Kiddush* of Shabbat we set apart a period of *time* as holy, in *Kiddushin* husband and wife set each other apart. Jewish tradition considered the woman who married as *mekudeshet*—"made holy," set aside and apart for her husband, consecrated and thus inviolate. In the view of Reform, this "setting aside" is mutual; both husband and wife are consecrated to each other. They create a sacred entity in the act of *Kiddushin*—consecration.

In the Jewish marriage service, in the very act of consecrating a *particular* relationship as holy, the potential sanctity of *all* relationship is asserted. Husband and wife represent the bond between God and humanity, the ideal toward which all human relationships should strive. *Kiddushin* is the rooting of the human in the realm of the sacred, with the goal that all our relationships become holy, bearing the blossom and fruit of life.

A Jewish marriage, then, takes place when a man and a woman, in the presence of at least two adult, competent witnesses, make a commitment to one another that their union will be inviolate. Each says to the other: "Behold, you are consecrated to me . . . according to the tradition of Moses and Israel." It is as if each were saying to the other: "I will do everything that I can to make our relationship sacred."

Since Judaism looks affirmatively upon marriage, including its physical aspect, *Kiddushin* is not "given" as a concession or as a required channel of salvation. Nor, strictly speaking, does a rabbi "marry" a couple; the bride and the groom marry one another. Because of the dignity and joy of this most important personal religious observance in Judaism, the rabbi is asked to speak the blessings in behalf of the community. But he does not "do" the *Kiddushin*. He is, in the careful rabbinic definition, the *mesadder Kiddushin*, the one who "arranges *Kiddushin*" and helps the couple through their act of consecration one to the other, as they begin together to form the sacred relationship of marriage.

Traditional Jewish worship was designed around the three overarching biblical motifs of Creation, Redemption (Exodus), and Revelation (Sinai). The entire round of Jewish observance is suffused by these same three themes. Thus, in the holiday cycle, Rosh Hashanah is clearly associated with Creation; Passover with the Exodus; Shavuot with Sinai. For *Kiddushin,* the act of marriage, the rabbis of our classic period chose the theme of Creation around which to design the celebratory blessings. These are known in our tradition as the *Sheva Berachot,* the Seven Blessings of Praise.

Indeed the *Sheva Berachot* contain in brief compass the entire sweep of the Jewish conception of existence, from the miraculous glory of the original panoply of Creation to the sublime perfection of Creation in the Messianic Completion. Both the evocation of Paradise and the affirmation of the messianic celebration are comprised in a seven-versed poem on the theme of Creation, which bears the luster of that crystallization which is the mark of poetry of genius. Even the *number* of blessings, *seven,* which is the numerical symbol of the cosmos, emblematic of the seven days of Creation, of the spheres, of light (the *menorah*), is meant to convey the unified theme of Creation.

Of the three major motifs of biblical Judaism, why did the rabbis choose the theme of Creation for the blessings of *Kiddushin?* Undoubtedly, first, because the miracle of Creation is renewed in procreation. Out of the very substance and spirit of husband and wife, created in the image of God, is spun the perpetual, miraculous fabric of life. Also, for the couple, a new life, a new world, does, in marriage, come into being. That is why, in the Jewish folkloristic conception, husband and wife are as newborn in marriage; they are, as it were, sinless, blessed with a whole new start in life.

Further, the purpose of Jewish existence is the partnership with God in the maintenance, the harmonization, of Creation. And every good marriage is considered to be a *tikkun,* a "putting in order," for each good marriage lifts existence to a state of higher harmony. Within the tradition, especially among the mystics, can be found the idea that every true act of love in marriage is itself a *tikkun*, uniting the transcendent and immanent aspects of Divinity, an analogy to spiritual and physical union in married love.

Thus, the consecration of a marriage is a cause for great rejoicing. Of all relationships, the marriage relationship is *kodesh kodashim*—the holy of holies, and the wedding, among all the rejoicings of life, is the *simchat semachot*—the celebration of celebrations. Indeed, in traditional Jewish life, the union of two lives was the occasion for celebration by the entire community. It is as if the framers of the wedding service gathered from the garden of the Hebrew language a whole cluster of words signifying happiness and joy, and put them together in the blessings, like a floral bouquet for bride and groom; "joy and gladness, mirth and exultation, pleasure and delight . . ." And again: "We praise You, O God, who brings joy to bridegroom and bride." And again: "And make the bridegroom greatly to rejoice with his bride even as You gladdened Your first creatures in Eden . . ."

And yet, while certainly expressing an ethos of pleasure in life, the *Sheva Berachot* do not encourage the couple to relinquish social obligations or, through self-isolating privatism, to endeavor escape from the ills of the world. The text of the blessings also evokes the messianic hope. The couple is encouraged to look beyond their private Eden toward the vision of Zion rejoicing with *all* her children. In the reference toward the end of the blessings to Jeremiah's vision (33:10–11), which sees beyond the terrors of the world to the ultimate wedding celebration in the peace of Zion, the couple are reminded of the Jewish commitment to the work of redemption for all.

As the couple begin to create their own world, they know that together they must bring something to the perfection of God's Creation, so that the time may soon come when God, as it were, will rejoice with His bride, the people of Israel.

—Herbert Bronstein

A JEWISH VIEW OF SEXUALITY

> It is *mitzvah* for a man and a woman, joined together in
> *Kiddushin*, to take pleasure in sexual union . . .
> "Marriage and the Jewish Home," *A–6*

JUDAISM does not project asceticism as an ideal. Pleasure, especially sexual pleasure, has a legitimate and important role in the life of the Jew. The Jewish view is that the pleasures of this world are a gift from God, and to renounce them is to show ingratitude to the Creator of the Universe. "A person will be held accountable to God for refusing to enjoy those pleasures that are permitted" (Talmud J., *Kiddushin* 4:12; see also note 43 above). A similar position was expressed by Maimonides: "One might say, inasmuch as jealousy, passion, love of honor . . . bring about a person's downfall, I will refrain from meat, wine, or marriage, or a pleasant home, or attractive garments. . . . This is an evil way and forbidden. He who follows these practices is a sinner" (*Yad, Deot* 3:1).

The Rabbis recognized the strength and importance of the human sex drive, while identifying it with the *yetzer ha-ra* (the evil inclination). It was called evil because it was easily subject to abuse, yet it was, at the same time, the energizing force in life. "Were it not for the evil inclination, no person would build a house, take a wife, beget a child, or engage in business" (Midrash, *Bereishit Rabbah* 9:9). The drives and passions of the human being were not seen by the Rabbis as inherently bad; they are good or bad depending upon the way they are used. The goal of Judaism is to sanctify every aspect of life.

This attitude is made explicit in the *Iggeret Ha-Kodesh*, which is attributed to Nachmanides (13th cent.):

> Know that sexual intercourse is holy and pure when it is carried on properly, in the proper time and with the proper intentions. No one should claim that it is ugly or unseemly. God forbid! For intercourse is called "knowing" and not in vain is it called thus. . . . we who have

the Torah and believe that God created all in His wisdom [do not believe that He] created anything inherently ugly or unseemly. If we were to say that intercourse is repulsive then we blaspheme God who made the genitals. . . . Hands that can write a Sefer Torah are then honorable and exalted; hands, too, can perform evil deeds and then they are ugly. So the genitals. . . . Whatever ugliness there is comes from how a man uses them. All organs of the body are neutral; the use made of them determines whether they are holy or unholy. . . . Therefore marital intercourse, under proper circumstances, is an exalted matter. . . . Now you can understand what our Rabbis meant when they declared that when a husband unites with his wife in holiness, the Divine Presence abides with them. (*Iggeret Ha-Kodesh*, as quoted by D. Feldman, *Birth Control in Jewish Law*, pp. 99–100).

The exalted role of marital intercourse under proper circumstances is further demonstrated by the notion that among the most appropriate times for it to take place is Friday night. "Understand, therefore, that the pious have not selected the weekdays, on which physical activity predominates, for their marital relations. They prefer the Sabbath which is spiritual, holy unto the Lord" (*ibid.*). The sex act thus becomes a holy act performed by the pious person at a holy time.

Judaism does not deny the rightness or the pleasure of sexual relations, but exalts them to the level of holiness. But to attain this level of sanctity, sexual intercourse requires the proper context. Jewish tradition condemns the use of force, coercion, or exploitation in sex. People are expected to conduct themselves in such manner as to reflect and radiate the divine image in which they were created.

Our society is undergoing a revolution in its sexual attitudes. The development of simple, effective, and inexpensive methods of birth control has made it possible to separate the fear of pregnancy from sexual intercourse. The women's movement is having a significant effect on the way women (and, for that matter, men) view themselves, their roles, and their bodies. The institutions of marriage and the family are being forced to respond to new conditions and new values. Sociologists are describing and advocating "alternative" life styles and different marital arrangements.

Living in a free society, then, in the closing decades of the twentieth century, individuals are faced with basic moral decisions about life-style options. While it is beyond the scope of this essay to explore any of these options in detail, it is essential to understand that, as Jews, we have certain definite notions about the worth and dignity of the individual. We also have responsibilities which extend to the Jewish people and humanity as a whole. In choosing life-style options for ourselves, therefore, we should always seek those which maximize human fulfillment and potential in the context of *kedushah*—holiness. That which distinguishes human beings from all other creatures is their ability to choose between good and evil.

In attempting to choose a sex ethic, one needs to explore the alternatives. Eugene Borowitz, in his *Choosing a Sex Ethic*, offers four possibilities: (1) the ethics of healthy orgasm, (2) the ethics of mutual consent, (3) the ethics of love, and (4) the ethics of marriage. In a detailed discussion Borowitz explores the implications of each possibility, and in extensive notes he offers much relevant material from Jewish sources. Borowitz notes that "the linkage of intercourse with marriage concentrates on the human value of sex, its significance for the family, the Jewish people and, therefore, human history" (p. 107). While Borowitz exhibits an openness to the ethics of love as a criterion for sexual intercourse, he concludes,

> Thus, the most ethical form of human relationship I know is love-for-life. Its appropriate social and religious structure is the monogamous marriage. This being so, marriage is, if I may use the strange formulation of ethical pluralism, the most right context, that is, the best criterion for the validity of sexual intercourse. And I think every human being should try to reach the highest possible level of ethical behavior (pp. 113–14).

It is not easy to legislate or to generalize ethics. Ethical decisions are made in concrete existential situations; they are made by human beings and not by statistics. Judaism, above all, recognizes the distinctiveness of every human being created in the image of God and his/her distinctive needs and drives. Yet recognizing all of this, it is quite clear that in

Judaism sexual intercourse is most appropriate and most ethical in the context of *Kiddushin*—sacred matrimony.

The following are suggested for further study: Eugene Borowitz, *Choosing a Sex Ethic* (New York, 1969); Louis Epstein, *Sex Laws and Customs in Judaism* (New York, 1958); David Feldman, *Birth Control in Jewish Law* (New York, 1968); and Samuel Glasner, "Judaism and Sex," in Ellis and Abarbanel, *The Encyclopedia of Sexual Behavior* (New York, 1961).

◆ ◆

KASHRUT

A REFORM POINT OF VIEW

> Many Reform Jews observe certain traditional dietary disciplines as a part of their attempt to establish a Jewish home and life style. For some, traditional *kashrut* will enhance the sanctity of the home and be observed as a *mitzvah;* for some, a degree of *kashrut* . . . may be meaningful; and still others will find nothing of value in *kashrut.*
>
> "Marriage and the Jewish Home," *E–6*

No guide for Jewish living would be complete if it failed to address the issue of *kashrut*, i.e., the fitness of certain foods according to Jewish tradition. *Kashrut* has been a basic part of Judaism for too long to be ignored; its role in the life of the Jew and in Jewish history ought not be underestimated. The home in Jewish tradition is the *mikdash me-at* (small sanctuary) and the table is the *mizbei-ach* (altar);* it is reasonable, therefore, to ask the Reform Jew to study and consider *kashrut* so as to develop a valid personal position.

Judaism has always recognized a religious dimension to the consumption of food. Being a gift of God, food was never to be taken for granted. And if this was true of food generally, it was especially true of meat, fish,

* See "Marriage and the Jewish Home," *E–1* and *E–7*.

and fowl, which involve the taking of life. And so it is not surprising to find literally scores of passages in the Torah* and the later rabbinic literature specifying which foods are permitted, which forbidden, and how they are to be prepared.

Kashrut—generally translated as "the dietary laws"—involves a whole series of food disciplines which range from the avoidance of pork and shellfish to the eating of *matzah* on Pesach. (It should be noted that there is a wide gamut of Jewish dietary observance which is unrelated to *kashrut*, from the major prohibition against eating on Yom Kippur to such minor customs as eating *blintzes* on Shavuot, *hamantaschen* on Purim, and *latkes* on Chanukah.) Jewish tradition considered *kashrut* to be an especially important part of the code that set Israel apart as a "holy people." Maimonides viewed *kashrut* as a discipline. "It accustoms us to restrain both the growth of desire and the disposition to consider the pleasure of eating and drinking as the end of man's existence." For many centuries it was *kashrut* which most conspicuously separated the Jew from the Diaspora society in which he/she lived.

The Reform movement has, for the most part, ignored the question of the relevance of the dietary laws. W. Gunther Plaut writes of *kashrut*: "the almost total silence of Reform literature on this subject is witness to the fact that it no longer was of real concern to the liberal leadership."† The Reform position was set out in the Pittsburgh Platform of 1885: "We hold that all such Mosaic and Rabbinical laws as regulate diet, priestly purity, and dress originated in ages and under the influence of ideas altogether foreign to our present mental and spiritual state. They fail to impress the modern Jew with a spirit of priestly holiness; their observance in our days is apt rather to obstruct than to further modern spiritual elevation." Although this blanket rejection of the dietary laws as outmoded represented the "official" position of the Reform movement through most of a century, it did not prevent individual Reform Jews and Reform congregations from adopting certain of the dietary laws for a variety of reasons, including the desire not to offend traditional relatives or guests.

---

* The basic biblical passages on *kashrut* are Leviticus 11 and Deuteronomy 14.
† W. Gunther Plaut, *The Growth of Reform Judaism,* p. 265.

The basic features of the traditional dietary laws are: (1) all fruits and vegetables are permitted and may be eaten with either dairy or meat dishes; (2) any type of fish that has fins and scales is permitted; (3) domestic fowl are permitted but birds of prey are prohibited; (4) all domestic animals which have both a split hoof and chew their cud are permitted; (5) meat and milk may not be eaten together, and the utensils used to prepare and serve meat or milk foods must be kept separate; and (6) fowl and animals which are permitted must be slaughtered and prepared for eating according to ritual law.

In attempting to evolve a personal position on *kashrut*, the Reform Jew or the Reform Jewish family should understand that there are several options, e.g., abstention from pork products and/or shellfish, or perhaps adding to this abstention the separation of milk and meat; these practices might be observed in the home and not when eating out, or they might be observed all the time. Or one might opt to eat only kosher meat or even to adopt some form of vegetarianism so as to avoid the necessity of taking a life. (This would be in consonance with the principle of *tzaar baalei chayim*—prevention of pain or cruelty to animals.) The range of options available to the Reform Jew is from full observance of the biblical and rabbinic regulations to total nonobservance. Reform Judaism does not take an "all or nothing" approach.

In the Torah (Leviticus 11:44 and Deuteronomy 14:21) the Jewish people is commanded to observe the dietary laws as a means of making it *kadosh*—holy. Holiness has the dual sense of inner hallowing and outer separateness. The idea of sanctifying and imposing discipline on the most basic and unavoidable act of human behavior, eating, is one of the reasons that may lead a person to adopt some form of *kashrut*. Among the other reasons that one may find compelling are: (1) identification and solidarity with the worldwide Jewish community, (2) the ethical discipline of avoiding certain foods or limiting one's appetite because of the growing scarcity of food in parts of the world, (3) the avoidance of certain foods that are traditionally obnoxious to Jews, e.g., pork, which may provide a sense of identification with past generations and their struggle to remain Jews, (4) the authority of ancient biblical and rabbinic injunctions, and (5) the desire to have a home in which any Jew might feel free to eat.

One or more of these reasons as well as others might influence certain Reform Jews to adopt some of the dietary regulations as a *mitzvah*, while others may remain satisfied with the position articulated in the Pittsburgh Platform. However, the fact that *kashrut* was for so many centuries an essential part of Judaism, and that so many Jews gave their lives for it, should move Reform Jews to study it and to consider carefully whether or not it would add *kedushah* to their homes and their lives.

◆ ◆

A BASIC LIBRARY

FOR THE JEWISH HOME

> In keeping with the *mitzvah* of *Talmud Torah* . . . a Jewish home should have a library, and time should be set aside for the study of Torah.
> "Marriage and the Jewish Home," *E-5*

It is admittedly presumptuous to select a few dozen titles from the tens of thousands of volumes of Judaica produced by scholars over the centuries and to present them as the basic library for the Jewish home. These suggestions are offered, however, recognizing that there are glaring omissions from the past and that worthier titles will appear in the future, because we could not recommend the collecting of a Jewish library without offering some guidance.

It would have been much easier to compile a list of one or two hundred titles than this list of thirty-odd. But we wanted to put together a list that a person could actually find, buy, and put on a shelf at modest cost. Another characteristic of this basic library is that all of the books have been published since the 1950s. Their modernity does not necessarily make them the best books available in their subject areas, but they are all readable, current, and authoritative. The person who reads through this library will understand how Judaism developed and what it stands for today.

One final word: this library was selected with a definite bias. Well over half the books were written by scholars identified with the Reform movement and/or were published by the institutions of Reform Judaism. Clearly, that is our orientation and we recommend it wholeheartedly. Now, in the words of Hillel, "Go and learn" (Talmud B., *Shabbat* 31a).

BELIEFS AND VALUES

1. Baeck, Leo.
   God and Man in Judaism. UAHC, 1958.
2. Bamberger, Bernard.
   The Story of Judaism. UAHC, 1970.
3. Gittelsohn, Roland B.
   My Beloved Is Mine: Judaism and Marriage. UAHC, 1969.
4. Kushner, Harold.
   When Children Ask About God. Reconstructionist Press, 1971.
5. Riemer, Jack.
   Jewish Reflections on Death. Schocken Books, 1974.
6. Spiro, Jack D.
   A Time to Mourn: Judaism and the Psychology of Bereavement. Bloch, 1967.
7. Steinberg, Milton.
   Basic Judaism. Harcourt, Brace & World, 1967.
8. Steinsaltz, Adin.
   The Essential Talmud. Bantam Books, 1976.

BIBLE

1. Freehof, Solomon B.
   Preface to Scripture. UAHC, 1957.
2. Heschel, Abraham J.
   The Prophets. Jewish Publication Society, 1962.
3. *The Holy Scriptures*.
   Jewish Publication Society, 1955.
4. Plaut, W. Gunther, ed.
   The Torah: A Modern Commentary. UAHC. *Genesis* appeared in 1974; other volumes to follow.

CUSTOMS AND CEREMONIES

1. Agnon, S. Y.
   Days of Awe. Schocken Books, 1965.

2. Bial, Morrison D.
   Liberal Judaism at Home. UAHC, 1971.
3. Central Conference of American Rabbis.
   A Shabbat Manual. CCAR, 1972.
   Shaarei Mitzvah. CCAR, 1979.
4. Gaster, Theodore H.
   Festivals of the Jewish Year. Morrow, 1953.
5. Schauss, Hayyim.
   *The Jewish Festivals: From Their Beginnings
   to Our Day*. UAHC, 1969.
6. Schauss, Hayyim.
   The Lifetime of a Jew. UAHC, 1950.

HISTORY

1. Grayzel, Solomon.
   A History of the Jews. Jewish Publication Society, 1957.
2. Orlinsky, Harry.
   Ancient Israel. Cornell University Press, 1954.
3. Plaut, W. Gunther.
   The Growth of Reform Judaism. World Union for Progressive
   Judaism, 1965.
   The Rise of Reform Judaism. World Union for Progressive Judaism,
   1963.
4. Silver, Daniel J., and Bernard Martin.
   A History of Judaism. Basic Books, 1974.

HOLOCAUST

1. Dawidowicz, Lucy S.
   The War Against the Jews: 1933–1945.
   Holt, Rinehart & Winston, 1975.
2. Friedlander, Albert H.
   *Out of the Whirlwind:
   A Reader of Holocaust Literature*. UAHC, 1968.
3. Wiesel, Elie.
   Night. Hill & Wang, 1960.
   The Town Beyond the Wall. Atheneum, 1964.
   The Gates of the Forest. Holt, Rinehart & Winston, 1966.

ISRAEL

1. Hertzberg, Arthur.
    The Zionist Idea. Doubleday, 1959.
2. Sachar, Howard M.
    A History of Israel. Alfred A. Knopf, 1976.

LITURGY

Central Conference of American Rabbis.
1. *Gates of Prayer: The New Union Prayerbook I*. CCAR, 1975.
2. *Gates of the House: The Union Home Prayerbook*. CCAR, 1977.
3. *Gates of Understanding*. CCAR, 1977.
4. *Gates of Repentance: The New Union Prayerbook II*. CCAR, 1978.
5. *A Passover Haggadah*. CCAR, 1974

◆ ◆

DIVORCE IN JUDAISM

> Judaism has allowed divorce since earliest times, often on
> quite liberal grounds.
>
> "Marriage and the Jewish Home," *D–1*

DIVORCE has been recognized by Jewish law since biblical times. In the Book of Deuteronomy (24:1) we read: "When a man takes a wife and marries her, and it comes to pass that she finds no favor in his eyes, because he has found some unseemly quality in her, then he may write her a bill of divorce and give it in her hand and send her out of his house..."

This is the basic statement on divorce in Jewish law, and it provides that—

1. It is the husband's prerogative to divorce his wife. The Torah does not extend this right to the wife.

2. The act of divorce must be spelled out in writing. (It is called *Sefer Keritut*, literally, a document of cutting off. In the Talmud this document is called a *get*.)

3. The written document of divorce must be given into his wife's hand

4. The fact that a wife no longer finds favor in her husband's eyes or

that he finds some unseemly quality in her may constitute grounds, from the husband's point of view, for divorcing his wife.

The wording of this law caused a dispute between the School of Hillel and the School of Shammai as recorded in the concluding paragraph of the Mishnah *Gittin* (9:10). The School of Shammai interpreted the words "some unseemly quality" (*ervat davar*) to apply only to cases of marital infidelity. The School of Hillel, however, interpreted the words more broadly to mean that a wife could be divorced for reasons other than unchastity, "even if she scorched the soup," and Rabbi Akiba said, "Even if he found another woman fairer than her."

The Jewish law is according to the School of Hillel. The latter's position took into account the fact that the institution of marriage includes components other than the sexual, the principal ones being companionship and harmony of relationship. Jewish law, by adopting this position, set a course quite different from that still followed by some states, where until very recently adultery was the only ground for divorce.

Although the biblical divorce law clearly favors the husband, a degree of equality for the wife was already known in mishnaic times. Under certain conditions the husband could be compelled by his wife to grant a divorce. "The following are compelled to divorce their wives: a man who is afflicted with boils or a bad odor or who works with malodorous material or is a coppersmith or a tanner . . . " (Mishnah *Ketubot* 7:10). The Talmud extends the grounds upon which a woman could demand a divorce, and the direction of Jewish law in succeeding centuries continued to broaden the rights of women. Around the year 1000 Rabbenu Gershom of Mayence decreed that a wife, unless she was unfaithful, could not be divorced except of her own free will. And the traditional *ketubah* (see "Marriage and the Jewish Home," C-4) contains provisions for a fixed amount of money to be awarded to a woman upon her being either divorced or widowed. It thus served as deterrent to a man who would too hastily divorce his wife.

The complex mechanics involved in the deliverance of a *get*, the traditional Jewish bill of divorce, which it was incumbent upon a husband or his representative to deliver into the hands of his wife or her representative, was another method devised by the rabbis to afford as much time as possible for a couple to effect a reconciliation. Yet with all these protections afforded the Jewish woman in ancient and medieval times, it is clear that the woman, under the traditional laws of marriage and divorce in Judaism, was at a distinct disadvantage.

It is understandable, then, why Reform Judaism from its very inception has rejected the traditional *get*. The virtually complete dominance of the husband in Jewish law is based upon the theory, accepted in both the Bible and the Talmud, that the wife is the property of the husband. The *get* perpetuates this philosophy and is thus clearly unacceptable in the context of Reform.

Reform Judaism classifies divorce laws with all the civil laws "which were an important part of Jewish law when all of Jewish life, religious and secular, was governed by Jewish law. These civil laws are now under the principle of *dina d'Malchusa dina*, i.e., the law of the land is the law with regard to civil law. Similarly, divorce . . . must no longer be considered a religious matter but a civil matter."*

However, there are complications in the position taken by Reform Judaism, the main ones being the great frequency of marriages between Reform Jews and Orthodox or Conservative Jews in the Diaspora and the relationship of Reform Jewry to the State of Israel. As of this writing, the laws of marriage and divorce in Israel are under the authority of the officially recognized Orthodox rabbinate. This means that no remarriage can take place in Israel without the prior procurement of a satisfactory *get*. And it also means that children born of a second marriage, if the first marriage was not dissolved by a *get*, will be considered illegitimate and will be subject to serious problems when the time comes for them to marry. Thus if a Reform Jewish couple divorce civilly, and there is a possibility of either or both settling in Israel or marrying non-Reform Jews, they should give serious consideration to the advisability of procuring a traditional *get*.

To summarize the Jewish attitude toward divorce, although Jewish law has always recognized the necessity of the institution of divorce, it was considered a tragedy to be avoided if possible. When tensions arise in a marriage, the partners should seek counsel from the rabbi and other pro-

* S. B. Freehof, *Reform Jewish Practice,* vol. 1, p. 106.

fessionals. As we read in the Talmud: "If a man divorces his first wife, even the altar sheds tears" (*Gittin* 90b).

The text of the traditional *get*, which has remained substantially the same throughout the ages, reads as follows:

> On the . . . day of the week, the . . . day of the month, in the year . . . of the creation of the world, according to the number we reckon here in . . . , I, . . . son of . . . , who stand this day in . . . , the city situated on the . . . River, do hereby consent with my own will, without force, free and unrestrained, to grant a Bill of Divorce to thee, my wife . . . , daughter of . . . , who has been my wife from time past, and with this I free, release, and divorce thee, that thou mayest have control and power over thyself and from now and hereafter, to be married to any man whom thou mayest choose, and no man shall hinder thee from this day for ever more, and thus thou art free for any man. And this shall be unto thee from me a Bill of Divorce, a letter of freedom, and a deed of release according to the Law of Moses and of Israel.
>
> > . . . , son of . . . , witness
> >
> > . . . , son of . . . , witness

◆ ◆

JEWISH ETHICAL WILLS

> It is a *mitzvah* to prepare an ethical will—a *tzavaah*—for the moral edification of the family, particularly the children.
> > Death and Mourning," *A–7*

ONE of the Jewish classics of the early twentieth century is Israel Abrahams' *Hebrew Ethical Wills* (Jewish Publication Society facsimile edition, 1976). To introduce the subject of ethical wills, we quote from Abrahams' Introduction:

> The ethical will is in a sense a distinctive Jewish genre (going back to the days of the Bible.) . . . . The most operative of all texts in this con-

nection has been Genesis 18:9, where God says of Abraham: "I have known him (Abraham) to the end that he may *command* his children and his household after him, that they may keep the way of the Lord." This text has inspired many a Jewish parent in after centuries, and it has been made the basis of an actual rubric in modern Jewish codes. It has been held to enjoin on every father the bounden duty to leave moral exhortations for his children's guidance. This feeling is well brought out in the following Midrash. "Jacob felt that his end was near, and besought the divine mercy: 'Ruler of the World,' he cried, 'take not my soul until I have exhorted my children.' And his wish was granted."

Below are excerpts from a classic twelfth-century will in the Abrahams collection and from a nineteenth-century will in the archives of a Chicago congregation, and a recent ethical will in its entirety.

From the Ethical Will of Judah ibn Tibbon (Spain-France, 12th cent.)

... Therefore, my son! Stay not thy hand when I have left thee, but devote thyself to the study of the Torah and to the science of medicine. But chiefly occupy thyself with the Torah, for thou hast a wise and understanding heart, and all that is needful on thy part is ambition and application. I know that thou wilt repent of the past, as many have repented before thee of their youthful indolence. ...

Therefore, my son! Exert thyself whilst still young, the more so as thou even now complainest of weak memory. What, then, wilt thou do in old age, the mother of forgetfulness? Awake, my son! from thy sleep; devote thyself to science and religion; habituate thyself to moral living, for "habit is master over all things." ...

Well art thou aware, my son! that the companionship of the ungodly is noxious, that their example cleaves like the plague. O "enter not into the path of the wicked!" Loiter not in the streets, sit not in the highway, go not with him whose society is discreditable. ...

My son! Make thy books thy companions, let thy cases and shelves be thy pleasure-grounds and gardens. Bask in their paradise, gather their fruit, pluck their roses, take their spices and their myrrh. If thy soul

be satiate and weary, change from garden to garden, from furrow to
furrow, from prospect to prospect. Then will thy desire renew itself,
and thy soul be filled with delight! . . .

Show honor to thyself, thy household, and thy children, by providing
decent clothing, as far as thy means allow; for it is unbecoming for
any one, when not at work, to go shabbily dressed. Spare from thy
belly and put it on thy back!

Let thy countenance shine upon the sons of men; tend their sick, and may
thine advice cure them. Though thou takest fees from the rich, heal the
poor gratuitously; the Lord will requite thee. Thereby shalt thou find
favor and good understanding in the sight of God and man. Thus
wilt thou win the respect of high and low among Jews and non-Jews,
and thy good name will go forth far and wide. . . .

Therefore, my son! Strive to honor me and thee from this day onwards.
All the honor I desire is to be remembered for good because of thee
in life and death; that those who behold thee may exclaim: "Blessed
be he who begat this one, blessed be he who reared him!" For I have
no son but thee by whom my name may be recalled, and all my
memory and glory are centered in thee. Reward from God and renown
from men shall accrue to thee, in that thou continuest my name for
good! . . .

From the Ethical Will of Rabbi Liebman Adler
 (Germany-Chicago, 1812–1892)

. . . Those children who do not live too distant should, if the weather
permit, and if it can be done without disturbing their own domestic
relations, gather every Friday evening around mother.

My children, hold together. In this let no sacrifice be too great to assist
each other and to uphold brotherly and sisterly sentiment. Each deed
of love you do to one another would be balm to my soul. The example
of eleven children of one father who stand together in love and trust
would be to his grave a better decoration than the most magnificent
wreath of flowers, which I willingly decline, but leave to your judgment.

The small savings which I leave will come to you only after the death of your mother. I know you; I may trust that you will not meet in an unfilial way about possession and disposition. The heritage which is already yours is a good name and as good an education as I could afford to give. It does not look as if any one of you had a disposition to grow rich. Do not be worried by it. Remain strictly honest, truthful, industrious and frugal. Do not speculate. No blessing rests upon it even if it be successful. Throw your whole energy into the pursuance of the calling you have chosen. Serve the Lord and keep Him always before you; toward men be amiable, accommodating and modest, and you will fare well even without riches. My last word to you is: Honor your mother. Help her bear her dreary widowhood. Leave her undisturbed in the use of the small estate, and assist if there should be want.

Farewell, wife and children!

Another point, children. I know well you could not, if you would, practice Judaism according to my views and as I practiced it. But remain Jews and live as Jews in the best manner of your time . . .

Ethical Will of Rabbi Jacob J. Weinstein (Poland-Chicago, 1902–1974)

It was a custom in ancient times for the father to leave an ethical will together with the legal testament. I hesitate to follow in this fine tradition for fear of imposing my will on yours. The state of the world which I leave you hardly testifies to the wisdom of my generation or those immediately before. I would be remiss, however, if I did not warn your generation that in your anger and frustration, you fail to distinguish between the conventions that enshrine the past because it is the past and the traditions which have in them the seed of a more meaningful future. There is no single simple or automatic way in which one can learn the art of this discretion—but I sincerely believe that the history and teachings of Judaism contain implicit and explicit guidelines for achieving a viable synthesis between the tried values of the past and the liberating needs of the present and the future. This belief and the understandable, though inarticulate, loyalty to the choices of a lifetime compel me to urge you to consider well the rock whence you were digged.

The attrition of the tradition in my lifetime [is evident;] there is a real danger that it will disappear in your children's lives. I would consider this an affront to the principle of continuity and a loss of a fine family resource. I know I cannot impose my values and judgments on you, but I can and do request that you not let this heritage go by default but that you study it, participate in it and make your decisions on the basis of knowledge as well as sentiment. You will find that it may be a very real help in holding you together as a family.

As love becomes more ambient, less focused, more dependent on necessity and convenience, it will need the more elemental instinctive support of family affection, of common womb genesis. So hold fast to the family affection you have so far maintained and try to pass it on to your children.

Instead of any formal visiting of the grave, I would prefer that the family try to observe a family day in the month of June at which reminiscences of happy incidents be the order of the day, and some worthy cause be remembered in fulfillment of the admonition *Tzedaḳah tatzil mimavet*—Charity (or social justice) saves from death.

◆ ◆

THE MOURNER'S *KADDISH*

It is a *mitzvah* for mourners to recite the *Kaddish* prayer in memory of the dead . . .

"Death and Mourning," *D–7*

EVERY day thousands of Jews all over the world recite the *Kaddish*. Even Jews who are generally indifferent to religious ritual will take upon themselves the obligation to recite the *Kaddish* as an act of reverence and filial piety. Some will recite it three times daily at synagogue services during the year following the death of a loved one; some will recite it at Sabbath services; and many will recite it annually on the *yahrzeit* of their loved ones.

What is the origin of this beloved prayer? And what is its meaning? Why does it respond so obviously to the deep needs of the bereaved?

Originally the *Kaddish* had nothing to do with death. It was a brief doxology (praise of God), recited in the Aramaic vernacular by preachers and teachers at the conclusion of their lectures during the talmudic period. It was inspired by a passage in the prophets that foretells the ultimate victory of God and concludes with the words: "Thus will I *magnify* Myself and *sanctify* Myself, and I will make Myself known in the eyes of many nations, and they shall know that I am the Lord" (Ezekiel 38:23).

The original *Kaddish,* based on this messianic passage in Ezekiel, consisted simply of what is now its first paragraph: "Let the glory of God be extolled, let His great name be hallowed, in the world whose creation He willed. May His kingdom soon prevail, in our own day, our own lives, and the life of all Israel, and let us say: Amen." Those present at the lecture or study session would then respond "Amen! Let His great name be blessed for ever and ever!'" This, then, is the basic *Kaddish* prayer; it was not until post-talmudic time that the remaining three paragraphs that we find in the prayerbook today were added (see *Gates of Prayer,* pp. 629–30).

The idea that the recitation of *Kaddish* would help rescue the souls of the dead from Gehenna seems to have originated around the second century; there is a story to that effect told about Rabbi Akiba and a condemned soul who was allowed to enter Paradise only after Rabbi Akiba found his son and taught him to recite the *Kaddish* for his father (*Tanna Devei Eliyahu Zuta* 10:7).

The Mishnah teaches that "the wicked are punished in Gehenna for twelve months" (*Eduyot* 2:10), and elsewhere in the Talmud we read that "the dead are not forgotten until after twelve months" (*Berachot* 58b). And so people began reciting the *Kaddish,* particularly in memory of parents, for twelve months. However, in the Middle Ages the custom developed to recite the *Kaddish* for eleven months only so that it should not appear that one considered his parent so wicked as to merit punishment for the full twelve months (*Shulchan Aruch, Yoreh Deah* 376).

Reform Judaism does not suggest that the recitation of *Kaddish* will help the souls of the dead to escape punishment, yet the *Kaddish* has a deservedly honored place in the Reform liturgy. "It expresses faith in the everlasting God in the face of death and resignation to His will. It also betokens pious regard for the memory of the departed. As such it serves to strengthen both the religious sentiment and the ties of family union. The loved and pleasant in life are not wholly divided even in death . . ." (*Rabbi's Manual,* CCAR, pp. 147–48). The *Kaddish* also enables one to express hope for the time when grief, suffering, and pain will cease.

There is no basis in Reform Judaism for limiting the *Kaddish* to eleven months since the *Kaddish* is not considered a prayer of intercession. And so the Reform Jew generally recites *Kaddish* during the *shivah* period and the ensuing year and then annually on the anniversary of death.

Yitgadal ve-yitkadash shemei raba

This the profound praise of the living,
Praise for the generous gift of life.

Praise for the presence of loved ones,
    the bonds of friendship,
    the link of memory.

Praise for the toil and searching,
    the dedication and vision,
    the ennobling aspirations.

Praise for the precious moorings of faith,
    for courageous souls,
    for prophets, psalmists, and sages.

Praise for those who walked before us,
    the sufferers in the valley of shadows,
    the steadfast in the furnace of hate.

Yitgadal ve-yitkadash shemei raba

Praise for the God of our people,
    the Source of all growth and goodness,
    the Promise on which we build tomorrow.*

* This is one of the meditations before *Kaddish* in *Gates of Prayer*, pp. 625–26.

THE ADMISSION OF CONVERTS

JUDAISM welcomes all sincere converts without regard to racial or national origin or to their former religious faith.

The biblical laws which excluded certain peoples from admission to the community of Israel were declared obsolete early in the talmudic period (Mishnah, *Yadayim* 4:4). Tradition prescribed that prospective *gerim* (converts) be warned in advance of the many religious responsibilities Jews assume, but that candidates for conversion should not be unduly discouraged (Talmud B., *Yevamot* 47a). Jewish literature has much to say in praise of converts and records the names of many illustrious and pious *gerim*.

The *Halachah* requires male converts to submit themselves to *berit milah* (circumcision) or *hatafat dam berit* (the drawing of blood) and afterwards to *tevilah* (ritual immersion). It also makes *tevilah* obligatory for female converts. In 1893 the Central Conference of American Rabbis declared the initiatory rites of *berit milah* and *tevilah* unnecessary. It is sufficient for the prospective convert (*ger*) to declare, orally and in writing, in the presence of a rabbi and no less than two lay leaders of the congregation and community, acceptance of the Jewish faith and the intention to live in accordance with its *mitzvot*.

Nevertheless Reform Judaism recognizes that there are social, psychological, and religious values associated with the traditional initiatory rituals, and it is recommended that the rabbi acquaint prospective *gerim* with the halachic background and rationale for *berit milah, hatafat dam berit,* and *tevilah,* and offer them the opportunity, if they so desire, to observe these additional rites.

It is understood that just as the rituals of conversion (*giur*) are important, so the preparatory period preceding the conversion ceremony is also important. This is given a high priority and value by Reform Judaism. The length of the period of preparation is determined by the

This statement was issued by the Committee on Conversion of the Central Conference of American Rabbis in 1978.

rabbi, taking into consideration the time needed by the candidate for conversion to obtain the necessary understanding and appreciation of Judaism in order to make a free-will decision with respect to his/her acceptance of the Jewish faith and identification with the Jewish people.

The period of study should be reinforced by requiring and assisting the prospective convert's active participation in the various celebrations, observances, and worship services of Judaism and the Jewish people. Regular attendance at synagogue worship, as well as evidence of concern for Jewish values and causes in the home and community, should be required. This is intended to enable the rabbi and his associates to satisfy themselves not only that the candidate has a sufficient knowledge of Judaism, but of even greater importance, that the candidate is a person of sincere and responsible character, who is genuinely desirous of making a wholehearted commitment to synagogue affiliation and to the Jewish faith and people.

GLOSSARY

Agunah. "Chained woman." A woman whose husband has disappeared without divorcing her; according to Orthodox Jewish law, she is not permitted to remarry.

Aliyah. "Going up." The honor of being called to participate in the service, especially to assist in the reading of the Torah or Haftarah. (It has also come to mean immigration to Israel.)

Aninut. The period from the time of death to burial when the mourners prepare for the funeral.

Aramaic. A Semitic language, closely related to Hebrew, that was widely used in talmudic times.

Ashkenazim. (Adjectival form: Ashkenazic). "Germans." The Jews of Central and Eastern Europe and their descendants; certain Ashkenazic customs, such as those pertaining to the naming of children, differ from those practiced by the *Sefardim.*

Atzeret. The final day of the Sukkot festival, coinciding in Reform Judaism with the holiday of Simchat Torah. (Orthodox Jews observe two separate days.)

Aufruf. (From Judeo-German). The practice of the groom (and the bride, in Reform congregations) being called for an *aliyah* on the Shabbat prior to the marriage.

Aveilut. "Mourning." The traditional Jewish mourning practices. See *Aninut, Sheloshim, Shivah.*

Avodah. "Service." Traditional designation for the Temple ritual, applied to a major part of the Yom Kippur afternoon liturgy.

Bar/Bat Mitzvah. "Subject to *mitzvah*." The status of the thirteen-year-old who undertakes the performance of *mitzvot* for him/herself; the ceremony at which he/she is called to the Torah for the first time.

Bar-Onshin. "Subject to punishment." The traditional designation for one who is old enough to be answerable at law and responsible for his acts.

Bat. "Daughter of." An element in Hebrew personal names indicating one's parentage, e.g., X *bat* Y, X the daughter of Y.

Bedecken. (From Judeo-German). The custom of ceremonially veiling the bride before the wedding.

Beit Am. "House of the People." A traditional designation for the synagogue.

Beit Din. "House of Judgment." Term, in rabbinic sources, for a Jewish court of law.

Beit Kenesset. "House of Assembly." A traditional designation for the synagogue.

Beit Midrash. "House of Study." A traditional designation for the synagogue.

Beit Tefillah. "House of Prayer." A traditional designation for the synagogue.

Ben. "Son of" (Aramaic equivalent: *bar*). An element in Hebrew personal names indicating one's parentage, e.g., X *ben* Y, X the son of Y.

Berachah. (pl.: *berachot*). A blessing or benediction.

Berit. "Covenant." (Ashkenazic pronunciation, *bris*). The term is often used for *Berit Milah.*

Berit Milah. "Covenant of circumcision." The ceremony during which the foreskin of the penis is surgically removed and the male brought into the covenant of Abraham.

Bikkur Cholim. [The *mitzvah* of] visiting the sick.

Birkat Ha-Mazon. "Blessing of the meal." Prayers said after eating.

Birkat Kohanim. The "priestly benediction" expressed in three Biblical verses (Numbers 6: 24–26).

Chalitzah. "Untying." The act of renunciation by which a childless widow is released from marrying her brother-in-law, as prescribed in Deuteronomy 25: 5–10.

Challah. The special holiday bread, usually baked in a distinctive twisted or plaited form, that is served on Sabbaths and festivals.

Chanukah. "Dedication." Mid-winter holiday commemorating the re-dedication of the Temple in Jerusalem in 165 B.C.E. by Judah Maccabee following the successful Jewish uprising against Syrian domination. It is celebrated for eight days beginning on 25 Kislev.

Chanukat Ha-Bayit. "Dedication of the house." The service at which a *mezuzah* is affixed to the doorpost of a house.

Chavurah. (pl., *chavurot*). "Fellowship." An informal, usually small association, sometimes but not necessarily formed within a congregation, whose purpose is the enhancement of Judaism through prayer, study and the adoption of a more explicit Jewish life style.

Chevrah Kadisha. "Sacred Fellowship." Communal burial society; its members wash and prepare the body for burial in accordance with traditional Jewish funerary practice.

Chol Ha-Mo-eid. The intermediate days of the Pesach and Sukkot festivals.

Chuppah. The traditional bridal canopy, beneath which the marriage ceremony takes place.

Confirmation. Originally a substitution for Bar Mitzvah, it is today observed in Reform congregations, on or near the holiday of Shavuot, as a graduation from religious school.

Derech Eretz. "The way of the land." Good behavior; dignified conduct.

Devar Torah. "A word of Torah." A brief session of Jewish study.

Eirusin. "Betrothal." Originally separate from and preceding marriage, *Nisuin.* From the 12th century on, it became customary to perform both ceremonies together.

Erev Shabbat. "Eve of Sabbath." Friday, particularly the evening.

Gehenna. (From *Gehinnom*, valley south of Jerusalem). Metaphoric name for the place of torment reserved for the wicked after death; hell.

Gemilut Chassadim. Acts of practical kindness and benevolence.

Ger. (f. *Giyoret*). "Stranger." A convert or proselyte to Judaism.

Get. The traditional divorce document.

Giur. The process through which one becomes a Jew.

Giyoret. See *Ger.*

Hachnasat Orchim. [The *mitzvah* of] hospitality to guests.

Haftarah. "Conclusion." A section from the Prophetic books read on Shabbat and holidays after the reading of the Torah.

Halachah. "Walking," i.e., the way that one should go. Talmudic law; the final decision of the Rabbis on points of law.

Halvayat Ha-Met. "Accompanying the dead." The *mitzvah* of attending a funeral.

Hamantaschen. Three-cornered, filled pastry, eaten on Purim, reminiscent of Haman's pockets.

Ha-Motsi. "He who brings forth." The benediction recited over bread and before eating.

Hashkavah. "Laying to rest." Memorial prayer in the Sefardic ritual.

Havdalah. "Separation." The ceremony which marks the end of Shabbat and festivals.

Hazkarat Neshamot. "Recalling of souls." Also known as *Yizkor.* Memorial prayers recited on certain holy days.

Hesped. Eulogy in praise of the deceased.

Hillel. (The Elder, c. 1st. century B.C.E.). Greatest of the sages of the Second Temple period, and ancestor of a dynasty of patriarchs which held office into the 5th century.

Judah the Prince. (Latter half of the 2nd century C.E.). The editor of the Mishnah. Also known as "Rabbi."

Kabbalat Shabbat. "Reception of the Sabbath." The opening section of the Friday evening service consisting of psalms, songs and, in the Reform prayerbook, meditations.

Kaddish. "Sanctification." A prayer (written mostly in Aramaic) in magnification of God and identified particularly as the mourners' prayer.

Kadosh. Holy; set apart.

Kashrut. "Fitness." The term is most often applied to the traditional Jewish dietary laws, but it might also refer to the fitness of religious objects.

Kavvanah. "Intention." The devotion one brings to the performing of a *mitzvah.*

Kedushah. "Holiness." The Hebrew word has also the connotation of separation, setting aside.

Keriah. "Tearing." The act of cutting or tearing a garment or ribbon as a sign of mourning.

Ketubah. The traditional Aramaic marriage contract.

Kiddush. "Sanctification." Prayers said, usually over wine, to mark the holiness of Shabbat or the festivals. Also a general term for the festive table after a morning service on such days.

Kiddushin. "Sanctifications." Term used in talmudic times to designate the betrothal phase of the marriage process; now widely used as the designation for the combined *Eirusin* (betrothal) and *Nisuin* (marriage) which constitutes the current Jewish marriage ceremony.

Kippah. (or Yarmulke). Head covering.

Kisei Shel Eliyahu. "Elijah's chair." Seat traditionally, and sometimes still today, provided for the prophet Elijah at the *berit milah* ceremony.

Kohen. A member of the hereditary priesthood, descended, according to tradition, from Aaron, the first high priest.

Kwater. "Godfather"; and *Kwaterin,* "Godmother." Titles of honor at a *berit milah.*

Lag Be-Omer. Thirty-third day of the counting of the Omer period (falling on Iyar 18); a semi-holiday during the mourning period between Pesach and Shavuot.

Latkes. Potato pancakes served traditionally during Chanukah.

Maimonides. Rabbi Moses ben Maimon (1135–1204), also known by the acronym Rambam; the foremost Jewish thinker and rabbinic authority of the Middle Ages. His writings include the *Guide of the Perplexed*, the *Mishneh Torah* (also known as the *Yad*), and the *Sefer Ha-Mitzvot*.

Matzah. Unleavened bread eaten during Pesach and especially at the *seder*.

Matzevah. A monument or tombstone.

Mazel Tov. A traditional Hebrew expression usually translated as "good luck" or "congratulations."

Menorah. A seven-branched candelabrum.

Mesadder Kiddushin. "Arranger of the marriage." Usually refers to the rabbi who officiates during a wedding ceremony.

Messilat Yesharim. "Path of the Upright." Treatise on ethics by Rabbi Moses Chaim Luzatto (1707–1746).

Mezuzah. "Doorpost." A scroll with biblical verses, usually in a container, affixed to the doorpost of a Jewish home.

Minhag. "Custom." An observance passed down through the generations, often assuming the power of law.

Mikdash Me-at. "Miniature sanctuary." The designation given to the Jewish home.

Mikveh. "A collection [of water]." A pool or bath of clear water, immersion in which renders one ritually clean.

Milah. Circumcision (see *Berit Milah.*)

Minyan. The quorum of ten males required for certain prayers and services in Orthodox Judaism but not in Reform.

Mitzvah. (pl., *Mitzvot*). A commandment or good deed.

Mohel. Ritual circumciser who, either in conjunction with the rabbi or by himself, performs *Berit Milah.*

Nachmanides. Rabbi Moses ben Nacham (1194–1270), outstanding Spanish talmudist and philosopher.

Nichum Avelin. [The *mitzvah* of] comforting mourners.

Nisuin. The formal ceremony of marriage.

Omer. "Sheaf." The 49-day period between Pesach and Shavuot, during which certain aspects of mourning are observed, is called *sefirat ha-omer*, counting the *Omer* (see Leviticus 23: 9–16).

Oneg Shabbat. "Sabbath delight." Generally referring to the social gathering after a Shabbat evening service or to a study session and get-together on Shabbat afternoon.

Pesach. Passover. Spring festival commemorating the Israelite Exodus from Egypt, with the concept of freedom as its main theme.

Pikuach Nefesh. [The *mitzvah* of] saving a life.

Pidyon Ha-ben. "Redeeming the son." A ceremony observed by some on the thirty-first day after the birth of a first-born son.

Peru U-revu. "Be fruitful and multiply." The first commandment in the Torah (see Genesis 1:28).

Purim. "Lots." The holiday commemorating the deliverance of the Jews of ancient Persia from an anti-Semitic plot, through the efforts of Mordecai and Queen Esther (see Book of Esther).

Rashi. Rabbi Solomon Yitzhaki (1040–1105), the leading medieval Bible and Talmud commentator.

Rosh Chodesh. The first day of the month, according to the Jewish calendar; the time of the new moon.

Rosh Ha-Shanah. The Jewish New Year festival, initiating a solemn period of soul-searching and reflection that culminates in Yom Kippur.

Saadiah. The greatest scholar and author of the Geonic Period (6th–11th centuries) and leader of Babylonian Jewry; lived 882–942.

Sandek. The person who holds the child during the circumcision ceremony.

Seder. "Order." The family meal and home ritual for Pesach.

Sefardim. (Adjectival form: Sefardic). "Spaniards." Jews who derived from the Iberian peninsula.

Seudat Chatanim. "Meal for grooms." A festival meal in connection with the religious act of marriage.

Seudat Havraah. "Meal of consolation." The first meal after a funeral, usually prepared by friends for the mourners.

Seudat Mitzvah. "Meal of *Mitzvah.*" A feast of celebration on joyous religious occasions.

Shabbat. The Sabbath. The seventh day of the week, an occasion for rest and spiritual refreshment, abstention from the concerns of the workaday world, and participation in home and synagogue religious observances.

Shadchan. Marriage broker.

Shammai. (50 B.C.E.–30 C.E.) A great sage and contemporary of Hillel's who usually took a more stringent attitude toward the law than Hillel.

Shavuot. "Weeks." The early harvest festival also known as Pentecost.

She-heche-yanu. "Who has kept us alive." Key word in a special blessing of gratitude recited on Holy Days and occasions of joy.

Shekel. A monetary unit in ancient Israel.

Shelom Bayit. "Peace of the House." Family harmony.

Sheloshim. "Thirty." The 30 days of mourning after death, including *Aninut* and *Shiva.*

Shema Yisrael. "Hear, O Israel." The central affirmation of the Jewish liturgy; taken from Deuteronomy 6:4–9.

Shiva. "Seven." The seven-day mourning period following the burial of a close relative.

Simchah. Joy, happiness.

Simchat Torah. "Rejoicing over the Torah." The festival marking the annual completion and recommencing of the Torah-reading cycle.

Sofer. "Scribe." One who writes Torah scrolls and other religious documents.

Sukkot. "Booths." The autumn harvest festival. The name is derived from the practice of building a *sukkah*, or temporary dwelling, during the festival.

Taanit Yachid. A private fast day.

Tachrichim. The white linen garment which tradition prescribes as dress for the dead.

Tallit. Prayer shawl.

Talmud Torah. "The study of Torah." The *mitzvah* of Jewish study; the term is also applied to the school where one studies Torah and Judaica.

Tammuz. One of the months in the Jewish calendar, corresponding to June–July.

Teshuvah. "Return." Repentance, denoting a return to God after sin.

Tevilah. "Immersion." Purification by immersion in a *mikveh*.

Tipat Dam. "Drop of blood." A symbolic circumcision in which drops of blood are taken from the crown of an already circumcised penis.

Tisha Be-Av. "The Ninth of Av." The day which commemorates the destruction of the first and second Temples in Jerusalem as well as other calamities in Jewish history.

Tosafot. "Additions." A collection of comments on the Talmud, composed in 12th–13th century France, and printed in most editions of the Talmud opposite the Rashi commentary.

Tzavaah. An ethical will.

Tzedakah. "Righteousness." A gift given as an act of justice and moral behavior.

Tzedek. Justice, righteousness.

Tzidduk Ha-Din. "Justification of the judgment." A prayer spoken as an affirmation of faith and acceptance of the inevitability of death.

Unterfuhrer. The escort(s) of the bride and groom to the *Chuppah.*

Ushpizin. "Guests." A mystical invitation issued to the patriarchs and matriarchs of the Jewish people to join us in the *sukkah.*

Viddui. "Confession." The prayer prescribed by tradition when death is imminent.

Yahrzeit. The anniversary of a death.

Yarmulke. (Or *Kippah*). Skullcap.

Yetzer Ha-Ra. The evil inclination.

Yetzer Ha-Tov. The inclination to do good.

Yibbum. Levirate marriage. See *Chalitzah.*

Yiddish. Language of medieval origin developed by Ashkenazic Jews, and derived from German and Eastern European dialects.

Yizkor. "May God remember." See *Hazkarat Neshamot.*

Yom Ha-Shoah. "Holocaust Day." The 27th of Nisan, set aside as a memorial to the six million Jews killed in the Holocaust.

Yom Kippur. The Day of Atonement, a solemn day of fasting and prayer concluding the ten days of penitence that begin on Rosh Ha-Shanah.

Zemirot. "Songs." Special musical selections sung at table on Shabbat and festivals.

THE CLASSIC
TEXTS OF JUDAISM

APOCRYPHA and PSEUDEPIGRAPHA Known in Hebrew as "hidden" works, both terms refer to collections of inter-testamental literature, ca. 200 B.C.E. to 200 C.E., primarily of Jewish authorship. They are "hidden" by exclusion from the Hebrew canon. Books of the Apocrypha and Pseudepigrapha are included in some Christian Bibles.

ARBAAH TURIM A comprehensive compilation of private and public law, by Jacob ben Asher (1270?–1340), chiefly following the legal opinions of Maimonides and universally accepted as authoritative. The code served as the basis for Caro's monumental *Beit Yosef* and later his *Shulchan Aruch*.

GEMARA (Lit. Completion). A word popularly applied to the Talmud as a whole, or more particularly to the discussions and elaborations by rabbinic authorities of the 3rd to 5th centuries C.E. on the Mishnah. There is a *Gemara* to both the Babylonian and Jerusalem Talmuds, although not to all or to the same tractates.

MIDRASH The method of interpreting scripture to elucidate legal points (*Midrash Halachah*) or bring out lessons through stories or homiletics (*Midrash Aggadah*). "Midrash" is also the designation of a particular genre of rabbinic literature extending from pre-Mishnaic times to the 10th century. Taken together, the body of works known as "Midrash" constitutes an anthology of homilies consisting of both biblical exegesis and sermonic material. Among the more important midrashic works are *Midrash Rabbah* (separate works on each volume of the Pentateuch, c. 400–1000); *Tanchuma* (a group of homiletical midrashim edited later than c. 800); and the *Pesikta de-Rav Kahana* (a homiletic midrash, probably c. 500, on portions of scriptural readings for festivals and special Sabbaths). Among the *Midrashei Halachah*, dealing primarily with law as derived from the Bible, are the *Mechilta* on Exodus; *Sifra* on Leviticus; and *Sifrei* on Numbers and Deuteronomy. All were edited c. 4th–5th century C.E.

MISHNAH   The first legal codification of basic Jewish law, arranged and redacted by R. Judah ha-Nasi about 200 C.E. The Mishnah is the nucleus for all *halachah*, and contains the basic Oral Law as evolved through generations. The Mishnah is divided into six orders: *Zera'im* (seeds), *Mo'ed* (seasons), *Nashim* (matrimonial law), *Nezikin* (civil law), *Kodashim* (holy things), and *Tohorot* (ritual purity), each order being divided into separate tractates.

MISHNEH TORAH   An encyclopedic legal code in fourteen volumes, also called *Yad Ha-Chazakah*, by Moses ben Maimon (Maimonides; Rambam), 1135–1204. The Mishneh Torah covers all halachic subjects discussed in the Talmud and gives clear rulings where there are conflicting opinions.

RESPONSA   (Heb. *She-elot u-teshuvot*) Replies sent by halachic authorities to questioners who addressed them in writing. These cover every aspect of Jewish belief and practice and are the main source for the development of Jewish law since the close of the Talmud and a primary source for Jewish and general history. The writing of responsa continues to our own day in all branches of the Jewish community.

SHULCHAN ARUCH   (Lit. A Prepared Table). The basis for Jewish law today, by Joseph Caro (1488–1575), codifying Sephardic custom and to which was added Moses Isserles' *Mappah* (Tablecloth), codifying Ashkenazic custom. Usually referred to as the *Code of Jewish Law,* the *Shulchan Aruch* contains four main sub-divisions: *Orach Chayim, Yoreh Deah, Even Ha-Ezer* and *Choshen Mishpat.*

TALMUD   (Lit. study or learning). The body of teaching which comprises the commentary and discussions of the early rabbis on the Mishnah of R. Judah ha-Nasi. Divided into the same Orders and Tractates as the Mishnah, the Talmudic discussions are always printed together with their corresponding parts of Mishnah. The *Babylonian Talmud* is the interpretation and elaboration of Mishnah as developed in the great academies of Babylonia between the 3rd and 5th centuries, C.E., and is considered more authoritative than the smaller *Jerusalem Talmud,* developed in the great academies of Palestine before the 5th century. The *Babylonian Talmud* especially, as a storehouse of Jewish history and customs as well as law, has exerted an unparalleled influence on Jewish thought and is the foundation of Judaism as we know it today.

TANACH   The traditional Hebrew acronym designating the Hebrew Bible, composed of the initial letters of the words *Torah* (Pentateuch), *Nevi-im* (Prophets) and *Ketuvim* (Writings, Hagiographa).

TORAH   (Lit. teaching, doctrine or instruction). The scroll consisting of the first five books of the Hebrew Bible for reading in the synagogue. "Torah" is also used to describe the entire body of traditional Jewish teaching and literature.

INDEX